基于学科核心素养培养的

中职英语教学评价探索

主　编　傅渝稀

副主编　刘雪梅　罗　慧

编　者（按姓氏笔画为序）

向　静　刘雪梅　李英惠　余正平

张　莲　罗　慧　崔　艳　彭　倩

傅渝稀　曾雪懿

外语教学与研究出版社

FOREIGN LANGUAGE TEACHING AND RESEARCH PRESS

北京 BEIJING

图书在版编目（CIP）数据

基于学科核心素养培养的中职英语教学评价探索 / 傅渝稀主编 ；刘雪梅，罗慧副主编 ；向静等编. -- 北京 ：外语教学与研究出版社，2024.4
ISBN 978-7-5213-5210-8

I. ①基… II. ①傅… ②刘… ③罗… ④向… III. ①英语课－教学研究－中等专业学校 IV. ①G633.412

中国国家版本馆 CIP 数据核字（2024）第 081346 号

出版人 王芳
责任编辑 贺伟华
责任校对 孙其宁
装帧设计 锋尚设计
出版发行 外语教学与研究出版社
社　　址 北京市西三环北路 19 号（100089）
网　　址 https://www.fltrp.com
印　　刷 三河市北燕印装有限公司
开　　本 787×1092　1/16
印　　张 10
字　　数 176 千字
版　　次 2024 年 4 月第 1 版
印　　次 2024 年 4 月第 1 次印刷
书　　号 ISBN 978-7-5213-5210-8
定　　价 39.80 元

如有图书采购需求，图书内容或印刷装订等问题，侵权、盗版书籍等线索，请拨打以下电话或关注官方服务号：
客服电话：400 898 7008
官方服务号：微信搜索并关注公众号“外研社官方服务号”
外研社购书网址：https://fltrp.tmall.com

物料号：352100001

记载人类文明
沟通世界文化
www.fltrp.com

前言

《中等职业学校英语课程标准（2020年版）》（以下简称《课程标准》）明确指出，评价是英语课程的重要组成部分，是引导、监控、促成和诊断教学目标达成的保障。英语课程的评价应反映以人为本的教育理念，着重评价学生学科核心素养的发展；应采用科学的评价方式和方法，对教学过程实施有效监控，对学习过程和效果进行适时检测，不断完善教学，促进学习，保证课程目标的达成。

《课程标准》正式颁布后，我们对其进行了比较深入系统的学习，通过国家规划教材在课堂上贯彻落实其相关理念和要求，经过几年的实践和努力，已经取得了一些成效。但是在评价方面，特别是终结性评价中，其题型内容和检测点与以往相比并没有多大变化，仍旧以语言知识和语言技能为主，还不能适应《课程标准》的新要求，未能很好地突出职业教育特色及实践运用。为了充分发挥评价的反馈调控功能，进一步推动落实《课程标准》倡导的英语课堂教学改革，契合时代发展要求，我们对“基于学科核心素养培养的中职英语教学评价”进行了积极探索。

该书一共分为两个部分：高一篇和高二篇。高一和高二篇分别由“基于学科核心素养培养的中职英语教学评价检测解析”“探索符合新课标的检测任务内容专项范例”和“探索落实学科核心素养及体现课程育人价值的综合检测任务示例”组成。

本书编写的原则：

一、坚持目标导向

以习近平新时代中国特色社会主义思想为指导，全面落实有理想、有本领、有担当的时代新人培养要求，将社会主义先进文化、革命文化、中华优秀传统文化、国家安全、生命安全与健康等重大主题教育有机融入检测任务内容中，充分发挥课程思政元素的积极作用，增强其思想性。

二、坚持问题导向

全面梳理目前中职英语教学中的困难与问题，明确考查重点和任务，积极回应经济社会发展的新技术、新工艺、新成果，遵循学生身心发展规律，精选对学生终身发展有价值的考查内容，明确考查要求，增强检测任务内容的指导性和可操作性。

三、坚持创新导向

既注重一线教学的实践性，又注重评价检测的适时性。强化基于真实情境和真实意义的评价检测的综合性和实践性，凸显学生主体地位，推动育人方式变革，着力发展学生英语学科核心素养，增强检测任务内容的适宜性和时代性。

本书编写的特点：

一、润物无声，课程育人

注重将党的教育方针具体化、细化为本课程应着力培养的职场语言沟通、思维差异感知、跨文化理解和自主学习等学科核心素养，体现正确价值观、必备品格和关键能力的培养要求。

二、源于生活，强调实践

检测任务均基于真实的生活或职业情境，注重将问题与学生的生活和学习情境化，将解决实际生活问题与学科核心素养能力有机结合，体现学以致用。

三、优化内容，注重指导

检测内容精心设计、层层递进，兼顾英语教学听、说、读、写四方面知识，灵活链接了教材内容与真实生活或职业情境，指导教师明确了“为什么教”“教什么”“教到什么程度”，而且强化了“怎么教”的具体指导，做到好用、管用。

本书的编者全部是中职英语教学研究中心组成员和部分中职学校一线骨干教师。全书编写体系清晰，编写内容紧扣新课标和国家规划教材，充分体现了情境化命题，题材新颖，贴近时代、贴近生活、贴近学生，注重价值引领，充分发挥了英语课程的育人功能，从而落实立德树人根本任务。希望本书能为广大中职英语教师就如何开展符合新课标要求、基于学科核心素养培养的中职英语教学评价提供思路及参考。由于编写时间和水平有限，本书的编写仍有不足之处，请广大读者和同仁批评指正。

目录

高一篇

基于学科核心素养培养的中职英语教学评价检测解析

《中等职业学校英语课程标准（2020年版）》（以下简称《课程标准》）明确指出：评价应以促进学科核心素养的养成为目标，构建课程、教学、评价相统一的评价体系。评价要关注学生职场语言沟通、思维差异感知、跨文化理解和自主学习等学科核心素养的发展，应能全面反映学生英语学科核心素养的发展状况和应达到的水平。

高一的中职英语教学评价检测基于这个学段的国规教材及教学实际，根据英语课程目标，充分考虑英语学科核心素养的综合性和生成性，探索基于真实情境和具象意义的表现性评价，聚焦学生在学习后是否获得了应具备的职场语言沟通、思维差异感知、跨文化理解和自主学习等核心素养，力争使评价从知识本位转向关注学生全面发展，考查学生英语学科核心素养的发展状况，同时关注课程思政及英语学科的人文性和课程育人价值。

中职英语教学评价检测，通过创设生动真实的生活或职业情境，引导学生运用所学知识进行语言理解、语言表达和语言交互，让学生运用在英语教学中发展起来的职场语言沟通能力、思维差异感知能力、跨文化理解能力和自主学习能力去完成生活或职场任务，从而全面落实立德树人的根本任务。该检测由听、说、读、写四部分共12个任务构成，包含《课程标准》要求的“人与自我”“人与自然”“人与社会”三大主题范围，涉及饮食起居，校园生活，个人、家庭及社区生活，出行问路，体育运动，自然环境，灾害防范，环境保护，历史人物与事件，庆典、聚会等话题。“说”是语言应用、与人开口沟通的第一步，对应“职场语言沟通”素养。我们把“说”放在第一部分，从Task 1到Task 3，要求学生朗读词汇、对话和短文，内容包括谈论日常运动、学校生活和介绍饭店特色。第二部分是“听”，从Task 4到Task 6，从听句子到短对话和长对话，内容包括节日庆典、日常生活和餐厅打工。为了让学生尽快适应中职英语学科的学习，根据“最近发展区”理论，一年级的听力测试部分专门保留了初中阶段一直在训练的短对话。作为“过渡”题型，其一方面体现初高中衔接，另一方面也增强学生的学习信心，提高其适应性。第三部分是“读”，从Task 7到Task 11，涉及图表类和应用类文本阅读等五个任务，内容包括节日庆典、运动健身、防震减灾、交通出行、垃圾分类。第四部分是“写”，一个任务，即Task 12，内容为写一篇求职信。四部分难易比例为7∶2∶1，基础题占比70%，中等难度题占比20%，稍高难度题占比10%。

Speaking （Task 1–Task 3，共20分）

【题型分析】“说”的部分为学生设计通用的生活或职业场景，创设英语口语使用情境，引导学生进行英语口语互动交流，通过反复朗读潜移默化地培养语感，帮助学生形成优美的语言和动听的语调，达到职场语言沟通和跨文化理解的核心素养培养目标。

本部分有朗读词汇、朗读情景对话和朗读短文三个任务。它们聚焦不同主题，创设相应情境，内容由易到难，考查学生识读词汇、语句和语篇的能力。Task 1考查学生正确朗读词汇的能力，要求学生能正确清晰地发音。Task 2考查学生朗读短对话的能力，要求学生根据职业场景扮演角色，朗读角色对应的对话内容，能在情境中简要描述人物、活动、事件或经历等，促进其职场语言沟通能力的提升。Task 3考查学生朗读短文的能力，要求学生在有准备的情况下能就熟悉的话题进行简单陈述，提升其职场语言沟通能力和思维差异感知能力。

Task 1

You are a member of the sports club in your school. Now you are telling the new members what they can do in the sports club. Read the following sports loudly. (0.5×10=5 points) 你是学校体育俱乐部的一员，正在为新成员们讲解体育俱乐部的活动。请将以下运动大声读出来。

1. go swimming	2. play table tennis
3. do T'ai Chi	4. go jogging
5. play football	6. play badminton
7. do yoga	8. play volleyball
9. go hiking	10. do kung fu

【解析】本任务聚焦《课程标准》基础模块“学习与生活”的主题，紧贴“体育运动”的内容创设生活情境，要求学生以参与者身份进入情境，能够正确朗读与常见体育运动相关的短语，能就“体育运动”话题进行基本语言沟通和口语交际，促进其职场语言沟通能力的提升，同时帮助学生了解中国优秀体育项目和国外常见体育项目，达成跨文化理解的核心素养目标。

Task 2

You are Li Hua. You are talking about your new school with your friend Wei Fang. Read the conversation and tell her about your new school life. (5 points) 你叫李华，正在与你的朋友卫芳谈论你的新学校。请读出对话，告诉她你的新校园生活。

Wei Fang: Hello, Li Hua. Are you happy at your new school?

Li Hua: Yes. My new school is quite different. We have classes in school and we also have skill-training classes in workshops.

Wei Fang: Do you like doing that?

Li Hua: Yes. It's very interesting.

Wei Fang: Which class do you like best in the workshops?

Li Hua: I like the cookery class best. It's useful. We practise cooking different dishes in the workshops.

【解析】本任务聚焦《课程标准》基础模块“自我与他人”和“学习与生活”的主题，紧贴“校园生活”话题设计情境，要求学生扮演角色，以参与者身份进入情境，能够识读语句，朗读情景对话，谈论学校、课程、课堂活动，并对学校生活进行评价。在这一任务中，学生通过完整语篇进行语言沟通，达到口语交际目的，达成职场语言沟通的核心素养目标。

Task 3

You are Li Hua, a staff member in a theme restaurant. Now you are live streaming to introduce your restaurant. Read the note loudly. (10 points) 你是李华，一家主题餐厅的员工。现在你正通过直播向大家介绍你的餐厅。请大声读出你的介绍词。

Hello, everyone. Welcome to my live-stream. I'm your friend Li Hua. What do you like doing in your free time? Doing exercise, going shopping or eating delicious food? For me, I like having different kinds of delicious food. And today I'm going to introduce an amazing restaurant to you. It's a new theme restaurant on Bayi Street. The food here is very tasty. And it's good value for money. The atmosphere is so nice. It makes you relaxed. It's a great restaurant. Do you want to have a try here?

【解析】本任务聚焦《课程标准》基础模块“自我与他人”和“科学与技术”的主题，将“饮食起居”和“网络生活与安全”两个话题合并，设计直播介绍餐厅的情境，让学生以职业人身份进入情境，能够朗读语篇，能就餐厅的食物、地理位置、环境、价格等进行描述，能进行简单的互动对话。在这一任务中，学生通过完整语篇进行语言沟通，达到口语交际目的，达成职场语言沟通的核心素养目标。同时，介绍餐厅可以帮助输出中国特色饮食与饮食文化，培养学生的跨文化理解核心素养。

Listening （Task 4–Task 6，共20分）

【题型分析】“听”的部分为学生设计通用的生活或职业场景，让学生以参与者或职业人的身份进入情境，涉及“自我与他人”“历史与文化”“学习与生活”等主题。学生在创设的真实情境中，听音频获取信息，根据生活或职场任务的要求处理信息。本练习旨在考查学生获取信息的能力，以及对获取的信息进行分析、归纳、总结并得出结论或发表自己看法的能力。

本部分包含听句子、听短对话和听长对话三个任务。它们聚焦不同主题，创设相应情境，由易到难。Task 4是基础题，考查学生听简单语句并做出适当反应的能力，在具体情境中提升学生的职场语言沟通能力。Task 5属于中档题，考查学生从简短对话中提取时间、数字、主题等相关信息的能力，帮助学生通过筛选关键信息提升思维差异感知能力和自主学习能力。Task 6属于稍高难度题，考查学生理解长对话的主旨、辨别说话者的态度等语言运用能力，在对比、辨别和理解的过程中提升学生的思维差异感知能力、跨文化理解能力和自主学习能力。

Task 4

You are a student from Xinhua Vocational School. Now you are talking about the festivals of your country with your friend Tom, who comes from Italy. You are going to hear five questions. Listen carefully and respond. Each question will be read twice. (1×5=5 points) 你是新华职业学校的一名学生。你正给来自意大利的朋友汤姆介绍自己国家的节日。你将听到5个问题。请听提问并做出回应。每个问题读两遍。

Question 1: When is the Dragon Boat Festival this year?

(　　) 1. A. It's 5 o'clock.

B. 22 June.

C. 2000 *yuan*.

Question 2: What will you eat on the Dragon Boat Festival?

(　　) 2. A. A glass of soda.

B. A dragon boat.

C. *Zongzi*.

Question 3: What do you do with your friends during the Dragon Boat Festival?

(　　) 3. A. By bus.

B. Watch a dragon boat race.

C. They are so kind and friendly.

Question 4: May I join you?

(　　) 4. A. Yes, take your time.

B. Sure, we'd love to have you.

C. No, I am not.

Question 5: Who is honoured during the festival?

(　　) 5. A. Li Bai.　　B. Yue Fei.　　C. Qu Yuan.

【解析】本任务聚焦《课程标准》基础模块“历史与文化”的主题，紧贴“庆典”“聚会活动”话题设计生活场景，让学生以参与者身份进入情境，能够对听到的音频内容进行信息处理，并根据内容做出合理回应，达成职场语言沟通的核心素养目标。本任务是对中国传统文化的传播。学生通过练习，能进行基本的跨文化交流，能用英语讲述中国故事，达成跨文化理解的核心素养目标。

Task 5

There are five short conversations here. Listen to the questions carefully, and try to find the correct answer. Both the conversations and the questions will be read twice. (1×5=5 points) 听5个短对话，根据每个问题选择正确答案。对话和问题读两遍。

Woman: Lynn, what are you going to do after school today?

Man: I'm going to practise English in the English club. I like it very much.

(　　) 1. What club is Lynn in?

A. English club.　　B. Sports club.　　C. Dancing club.

Man: Good morning, Madam. May I help you?

Woman: Yes. I want to buy a dress for my daughter.

(　　) 2. What does the woman want to buy?

A. A cake. B. A dress. C. Some food.

Man: I will take the high-speed train to Beijing next week. It's cheaper than air travel.

Woman: Yes, it's a good choice if the journey is not too long.

(　　) 3. How will the man go to Beijing?

A. By air. B. By train. C. By bus.

Woman: Hello, this is ABC Company.

Man: Hello. This is Bruce White. May I speak to Mr Green?

(　　) 4. What are they doing?

A. They are chatting.

B. They are singing.

C. They are making a call.

Woman: I am interested in collecting stamps. What about you?

Man: I like playing basketball very much.

(　　) 5. What's the man's hobby?

A. Playing basketball. B. Going swimming. C. Watching films.

【解析】本任务聚焦《课程标准》基础模块的"自我与他人""学习与生活"和"社会交往"等主题，围绕校园活动、购物、交通出行、交流与沟通展开简短对话，内容灵活多样，要求学生能够对听到的音频进行信息处理，能够根据对话内容对每个问题做出正确回应，达成职场语言沟通的核心素养目标。本任务有对高铁的赞美，有中西方电话用语的差异等内容。学生在完成练习的过程中，可达成跨文化理解和思维差异感知的核心素养目标。

Task 6

You are Li Hua who is taking a customer's order now. Listen carefully and try to find the correct answer for each question. The conversation will be read twice. (2×5=10 points) 你是李华，正在为顾客点餐。请仔细听对话，并根据对话内容为每个问题选择正确答案。对话读两遍。

Li Hua: *Good evening. Welcome to our restaurant.*
Customer: *Good evening.*
Li Hua: *Are you ready to order now?*
Customer: *Yes, I'd like the vegetable soup first.*
Li Hua: *OK. What would you like as the main course?*
Customer: *Beijing Roast Duck, Sweet and Sour Pork and Mapo Tofu.*
Li Hua: *How about the staple?*
Customer: *Rice, please.*
Li Hua: *What would you like to drink?*
Customer: *Two bottles of orange juice and a glass of soda.*
Li Hua: *Anything else?*
Customer: *That's enough.*
Li Hua: *Wait a moment, please.*

(　　) 1. What does the customer want first?
A. Beijing Roast Duck.　B. Vegetable soup.　C. Rice.

(　　) 2. The customer wants ________ as the main course.
A. soda　B. cola　C. Mapo Tofu

(　　) 3. What staple does the customer want?
A. Noodles.　B. Rice.　C. Dumplings.

(　　) 4. What does the customer want to drink?
A. Soda.　B. Water.　C. Cola.

(　　) 5. How many dishes does the customer want as the main course?
A. Four.　B. Five.　C. Three.

【解析】本任务聚焦《课程标准》基础模块“自我与他人”的主题，紧贴“饮食起居”话题设计职业场景，要求学生以餐厅服务员的身份进入情境，询问顾客需求，根据顾客需求做出合理回应，提取关键信息，达成职场语言沟通的核心素养目标。本任务有对中国传统美食的介绍，引导学生介绍中国文化，通过基本的跨文化交流，达成跨文化理解的核心素养目标。

Reading （Task 7–Task 11，共50分）

【题型分析】“读”的部分为学生设计生活或职场常见的图表、文本等，让学生通过看图表、读语篇等阅读活动获取信息，并通过分析、梳理、归纳信息实现信息转换，完成生活或职场交际任务，达成职场语言沟通和跨文化理解的核心素养目标。本部分包含图表类和应用类文本阅读等五个任务，聚焦“庆典、聚会等活动”“体育运动”“灾害防范”“出行问路”“环境保护”等不同话题，创设相应情境，形式多样，内容丰富，难度适中。Task 7为看图片匹配文字题，要求学生能看懂图片并与相关信息进行匹配，提高职场语言沟通能力。Task 8为提取文本信息完成信息卡题，要求学生能从主题熟悉的文本中找到特定信息，完成计划表，增强自主学习能力。Task 9为根据表格信息补全语篇，要求学生能读懂常见的活动要素的表述并理解信息关联，完成短文填空，增强跨文化理解能力和自主学习能力。Task 10为交通出行类文本，要求学生提取信息并选择正确答案，增强职场语言沟通能力。Task 11为垃圾分类文本，要求学生能在文本中找出特定信息，根据主题熟悉的文本信息理解主旨，做出推论，增强自主学习能力。本部分可以促使学生留心身边的句子，训练学生提取语言信息的技巧，提高学生的自主学习能力。

Task 7

What do you do during the Spring Festival? Match the activities to the pictures. (2×5=10 points) 春节期间你都做什么呢？请将下列新年习俗与对应的图片配对。

A. paste spring couplets	B. have a reunion dinner
C. make paper-cuttings	D. get lucky money
E. set off firecrackers	

1. ______________

2. ______________

3. ______________

4. ______________

5. ______________

1. ______________ 2. ______________ 3. ______________
4. ______________ 5. ______________

【解析】本任务聚焦《课程标准》基础模块“历史与文化”的主题，创设春节情境，展示中国春节习俗，要求学生能看懂与节日相关的图片，理解相关的词汇，匹配与词义所展示情境相同的图片，完成练习。学生通过图片直观感受节日氛围，并用英语介绍和传播中国传统文化，达成职场语言沟通和跨文化理解的核心素养目标。学生在完成练习的过程中，形成文化自信，增强文化底蕴，提升学习英语的自信心，提高自主学习的能力。

Task 8

You are Li Hua, studying at a vocational school. You seldom took part in any sport before. But now you want to make a change. Read the following introduction and make a fitness plan for yourself. (2×5=10 points) 你是李华，一名职业学校学生。以前你不爱运动，但是现在你想做出改变。请阅读以下介绍，为自己做一份健身计划表。

My name is Li Hua. I am sixteen years old. I used to play video games and seldom took part in any sport. Besides, I liked fast food and soft drinks. But recently, I often feel tired all day and look pale. It's not good for me. I want to make some changes. Now

I go jogging for half an hour every day. And I play basketball two or three times a week. If I keep doing so, I'm sure I will lose 5 kg in three months and I will feel better.

Fitness plan	
Name	1. ________
Age	2. ________
Exercise	3. ________ for half an hour every day Play basketball 4. ________ every week
Fitness goal	5. ________ in three months and feel better

【解析】本任务聚焦《课程标准》基础模块“自我与他人”和“学习与生活”的主题，围绕“体育运动”话题创设情境，要求学生理解和提取语篇中相关信息，通过补全健身计划，完成相应的任务。本项练习主要考查学生对词、句的理解和通过略读提取信息的能力，培养学生读、写能力，达成职场语言沟通、跨文化理解和思维差异感知的核心素养目标。

Task 9

You are a volunteer working for earthquake prevention and disaster reduction. Complete the speech according to the chart below. (1×10=10 points) 你是一名宣传防震减灾知识的志愿者。请根据下面的图表完成宣讲稿。

Do's	Don'ts
· Use the stairs	· Jump from a high building
· Rush under the table	· Use the lift
· Keep away from the walls	· Take all your money
· Turn off the gas	· Get near the window

How to protect yourself

Good morning, everyone. I am a 1. ______________. Today I will tell you how to 2. ______________ yourself when an earthquake happens. 3. ______________, rush to the squares or ground. Don't take all your 4. ______________. Just rush downstairs and 5. ______________ (get) to the squares. Second, remember not to use the 6. ______________, use the stairs. If you can't go outside, rush 7. ______________ the table as soon as possible. 8. ______________ jump from a high building. Third, keep 9. ______________ from the walls. Don't get near the windows. If it's possible, 10. ______________ the gas. These are some ways to protect yourself. Please remember them.

【解析】本任务聚焦《课程标准》基础模块“自然与环境”的主题，创设志愿者进行防震减灾宣传的情境，要求学生以志愿者身份进入情境，能读懂防震知识的信息表，提取数字、事件、主题等特定信息，根据提示或关键词转述文本大意，补全文本内容。学生在理解重点词汇的基础上，能将其运用到整句表达中，介绍地震发生时的避险措施，达成职场语言沟通和跨文化理解的核心素养目标。

Task 10

You are a reporter of the school's radio station. You have asked 100 students how they go to school. Answer some questions to show your report. (2×5=10 points) 你是学校广播站的记者。为了了解同学们上学的交通方式，你采访了100名学生。请根据要求回答问题，向同学们说明你的采访情况。

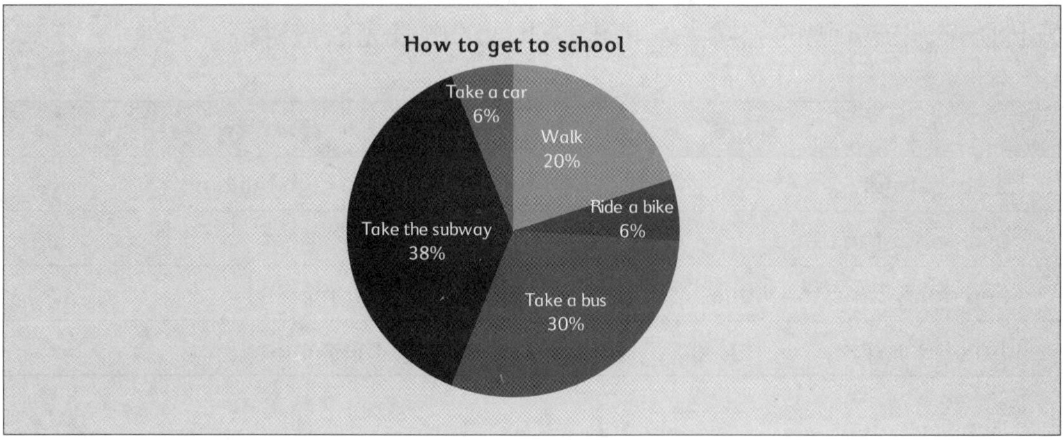

Some students go to school on foot because they live near their school. Some students go to school by bike because they live farther away, or because they like riding bikes. They think it's quick, convenient and good for their health. Today more people have cars, so they drive their children to school. It's cheaper to take a bus than take the subway. But in rush hour, it will take more time.

(　　) 1. ________ students take cars to school.

A. 6%　　B. 38%　　C. 20%

(　　) 2. According to the pie chart, most students ________ to school.

A. walk　　B. take the subway　　C. ride a bike

(　　) 3. If there are 2000 students in the school, how many students go to school on foot?

A. 120.　　B. 400.　　C. 600.

(　　) 4. Students walk to school because ________.

A. they like walking

B. it's quick and cheap

C. they live near their school

(　　) 5. Taking a bus is ________.

A. good for health

B. cheaper than taking the subway

C. most convenient

【解析】本任务聚焦《课程标准》基础模块“学习与生活”的主题，紧贴“出行问路”话题创设情境，要求学生以记者身份进入情境，能读懂饼图，找到比例、方式、主题等特定信息，理解采访内容，根据采访信息做出推断，完成答案选择。在读图表与采访的过程中，学生通过数据分析、语句理解，了解文章内容、观点等，达到英语交际目的和职场语言沟通、跨文化理解的核心素养目标，发展思维差异感知能力和自主学习能力。

Task 11

You are a volunteer of environmental protection. Now you're telling people how to sort rubbish. Answer the following questions according to your introduction. (2×5=10 points) 你是一名环保志愿者。你正在为人们讲解如何进行垃圾分类。请根据讲解内容回答相关问题。

Kitchen waste is a type of household waste, like leftovers, flowers and plants. It is heavy in weight. It is something you don't want but can be <u>composted</u>.

Paper, metal, glass, plastics and other things that can be reused are recyclable waste.

Harmful waste includes things like medicine and batteries.

The waste that is not kitchen, recyclable or harmful waste will go to the "Other waste" bin.

(　　) 1. According to the picture, rubbish is divided into ________ kinds.

A. three　　B. four　　C. five

(　　) 2. You can throw used paper into the "________" bin.

A. Harmful waste　　B. Other waste　　C. Recyclable waste

(　　) 3. Which of the following is harmful waste?

A. Metal.　　B. Glass.　　C. Medicine.

(　　) 4. Leftovers are ________ waste.

A. kitchen　　B. recyclable　　C. other

(　　) 5. What does the underlined word "composted" mean?

A. 做堆肥　　B. 重复使用　　C. 榨油

【解析】本任务聚焦《课程标准》基础模块“自然与环境”的主题，紧贴“环境保护”话题创设垃圾分类的场景，要求学生以志愿者身份进入情境，完成阅读长语篇的任务，读懂垃圾的主要类别，能够提取、梳理、归纳信息，完成选择。学生在情境中理解语篇内容，了解语篇的目的、内在的逻辑关系等，达成英语阅读理解目的以及职场语言沟通和跨文化理解的核心素养目标，提升思维差异感知能力和自主学习能力。

Writing（Task 12，共10分）

【题型分析】“写”的部分为学生设计常见的生活或职业场景，要求学生根据提供的信息或场景要求，完成写作任务。本部分包含一个任务，聚焦学生熟悉的生活或职业场景，涉及《课程标准》中的八大主题，以应用文类和记叙文类为主。学生能用简短语言介绍自己、家人或家乡，能简要介绍活动、事件、节日或经历等，能在对方帮助下记录简短信息，能写出简单的通知、请假条、求职信、个人职业规划等应用类短文，从而提升思维差异感知能力、跨文化理解能力和自主学习能力。

Task 12

You are Li Hua from Bright Vocational School. In the coming summer holiday, you're going to do a part-time job. Write an email to apply for a job. (10 points) 你是光明职业学校的一名学生，名叫李华。暑假即将到来，你想在暑假做一份兼职。请根据以下信息写一封求职信。

An introduction about Li Hua

Name	Li Hua
Age	16
Character	◆honest and easy-going ◆good at solving problems
Major	Computer Science
Hobbies	◆reading books ◆playing the guitar
Time for work	each afternoon, before 9:00 pm

Dear Sir/Madam,

I'm writing to apply for a part-time job. Please allow me to introduce myself. ____
____
____.

Thank you for your kind attention. Please let me hear from you as soon as possible.

Yours sincerely,

Li Hua

【解析】本任务聚焦《课程标准》基础模块“自我与他人”的主题，创设学生申请暑假兼职的情境，要求学生能读懂表格内容，并根据个人爱好、专业、工作时间等信息写一封求职信，帮助学生在写邮件的同时感受如何表达自我和与人沟通，增强跨文化理解能力和思维差异感知能力。

评价检测解析（基础模块一）写作范文

Dear Sir/Madam,

I'm writing to apply for a part-time job. Please allow me to introduce myself.

My name is Li Hua. I'm sixteen years old. I am an honest person. And I can get along well with others. At the same time, I am good at solving different kinds of problems. Now, I'm studying at Bright Vocational School. My major is Computer Science. And at school, I won the first place in the big data application competition. I like reading books, because I can learn some new knowledge from them. I also like playing the guitar. It can help me relax. I can work each afternoon before 9:00 pm.

Thank you for your kind attention. Please let me hear from you as soon as possible.

Yours sincerely,

Li Hua

二 探索符合新课标的检测任务内容专项范例

新课标理念下的口语专项检测范例

(一)

Task 1

You are Li Hua. You're talking to a friend about daily eco-friendly behaviour. Read the following sentences loudly. (0.5×10=5 points) 你是李华，你正在跟朋友谈论日常环保行为。请大声读出下列句子。

1. Use cloth bags.
2. Plant more trees.
3. Use public transport.
4. Turn off the light after use.
5. Save energy.
6. Save food.
7. Sort the waste.
8. Buy fresh, buy local.
9. Turn off the water while brushing teeth.
10. Don't leave computers on standby.

Task 2

You are Li Hua. You're discussing escape guidelines during an earthquake with your mum. Read the following conversation loudly. (5 points) 你是李华，正在跟妈妈讨论地震时的逃生指南。请大声读出以下对话。

Mum: Son, if an earthquake comes, what can we do to protect ourselves?

Li Hua: If we're at home, we should turn off the gas and electricity as soon as possible.

Mum: That's right. Can we use the lift?

Li Hua: No way. Use the stairs instead of the lift.

Mum: If it's too late to leave home, what should we do?

Li Hua: Take shelter under stable objects to protect ourselves.

Mum: Can't agree more.

Task 3

You are Li Hua, a vocational school student who is introducing your new school. Read your introduction loudly. (10 points) 你是李华，一所职业学校的学生，正在介绍你的新学校。请大声读出你的介绍内容。

> I'm studying at a vocational school now. Our school is quite different from an ordinary high school. We learn English, Chinese, maths, etc. in the classroom, and we have skill-training classes in workshops. Our teachers always give us lots of practical tips. They are very helpful. The skill-training teachers are very special, because they come from different fields. Some are workers in factories, others are chefs in restaurants... All of our teachers are not only knowledgeable and experienced, but also very kind and friendly. I'm sure I'll learn a lot from them.

（二）

Task 1

You are Li Hua. You're watching a documentary about natural disasters. Read the following expressions loudly. (0.5×10=5 points) 你是李华，正在观看一部介绍自然灾害的纪录片。请大声读出下列表述。

1. flood	2. drought	3. earthquake	4. typhoon
5. rainstorm	6. sandstorm	7. heavy fog	8. wildfire
9. lightning	10. Black Death		

Task 2

You are Li Hua. You are sharing some tips about daily eco-friendly behaviour with Zhou Bo. Read the following conversation loudly. (5 points) 你是李华，正在跟你的同学周博分享日常环保行为。请大声读出下列对话。

Li Hua: Zhou Bo, do you have any good ideas to improve air quality?

Zhou Bo: I think we'd better use electric cars.

Li Hua: I think so. And it is also a good way to use public transport.

Zhou Bo: Yes, that can make the air cleaner.

Li Hua: Planting more trees is of great help, too.

Zhou Bo: Can't agree more.

Task 3

You are Li Hua, a volunteer who is introducing some self-protection tips during an earthquake to kids in a kindergarten. Read your introduction loudly. (10 points) 你是李华，一名志愿者，正在向幼儿园的小朋友们介绍地震逃生指南。请大声读出你的介绍内容。

> Hello, little friends! Today we are going to talk about earthquakes. First, let's watch a video about earthquakes... Now we have known some information about earthquakes. It can be a little scary, but if we know what to do, we can keep ourselves safe. The first thing to remember is "Drop, cover, and hold on". That means if you feel the ground shaking, you should drop to the ground, find something like a stable object to cover yourself, and hold on to it tightly. This will help protect you from falling objects. Second, don't use the lift, which is very dangerous. Last but not least, you must listen to your teachers or parents. They will help you and tell you how to protect yourselves.

新课标理念下的听力专项检测范例

（一）

Task 1

You are a fresh student of a vocational school. Now you are talking about your new school with your friend. You are going to hear five questions from your friend. Listen carefully and respond. Each question will be read twice. (1×5=5 points) 你是一所职业学校的新生，正跟你的朋友谈论你的新学校。你会听到朋友的5个问题。请听提问并做出回应。每个问题读两遍。

(　　) 1. A. Yes, please.
B. Yes, my new school is quite different.
C. Yes, I don't like the new school.

(　　) 2. A. We have skill-training classes in workshops.
B. We have classrooms.
C. We have a playground.

(　　) 3. A. We can learn how to operate different machines.
B. We can learn Chinese.
C. We can play basketball.

(　　) 4. A. The library.
B. The teachers.
C. Mechanical basics.

(　　) 5. A. Because it's interesting and useful.
B. Because it's difficult and boring.
C. Because we can taste what we cook.

Task 2

There are five short conversations here. Listen to the questions carefully, and try to find the correct answer. Both the conversations and the questions will be read twice. (1×5=5 points) 听5个短对话，根据每个问题选择正确答案。对话和问题读两遍。

(　　) 1. How will the woman most probably go to the nearest subway station?
A. By bus.　　B. On foot.　　C. By taxi.

(　　) 2. How did the woman and Lynn become friends?
A. They were classmates.
B. They have the same hobby.
C. They have the same photo.

(　　) 3. What season is it?
A. Spring.　　B. Autumn.　　C. Winter.

(　　) 4. Which festival are they talking about?
A. The Spring Festival.
B. The Mid-Autumn Festival.
C. The Lantern Festival.

(　　) 5. Does Tim eat takeaways now?

A. Yes.　　B. No.　　C. Don't know.

Task 3

Joe is ordering food. Listen carefully and try to find the correct answer for each question. The conversation will be read twice. (2×5=10 points) 乔正在点餐。请仔细听对话，并根据对话内容为每个问题选择正确答案。对话读两遍。

(　　) 1. Where did the conversation happen?

A. At a restaurant.　　B. In a hotel.　　C. On the street.

(　　) 2. Did the customer decide what to order at first?

A. Yes.　　B. No.　　C. Not mentioned.

(　　) 3. What is "Yu Xiang Rou Si"?

A. It's fish-flavored pork slices.

B. It's a kind of fish.

C. It's the name of the waiter.

(　　) 4. How many dishes did the customer order?

A. One.　　B. Two.　　C. Three.

(　　) 5. What drink did the customer order?

A. A glass of water.

B. A glass of milk.

C. A glass of orange juice.

(二)

Task 1

Nancy is an overseas student who is studying in China. She is now doing an interview about the Mid-Autumn Festival. As an interviewee, you are supposed to answer five questions from Nancy. Listen carefully and respond. Each question will be read twice. (1×5=5 points) 南希是一名留学生，她正在做一个关于中秋节的调研采访。你作为采访对象，需要回答南希的5个问题。请仔细听提问并做出回应。每个问题读两遍。

(　　) 1. A. On the 15th day of the eighth lunar month.
B. On the first day of each year of the Chinese lunar calendar.
C. On the ninth day of the ninth lunar month.

(　　) 2. A. We hang lanterns on the streets and in the parks.
B. We will travel this year.
C. We often eat mooncakes and appreciate the full moon.

(　　) 3. A. It is round with fillings in the centre.
B. It is shared among family and friends.
C. It is a symbol of reunion.

(　　) 4. A. We have a family reunion dinner together.
B. We set off firecrackers.
C. We give lucky money.

(　　) 5. A. Well, I plan to put up spring couplets.
B. Well, I plan to celebrate the day with my classmates. We are going to have a party.
C. Well, I plan to celebrate the New Year.

Task 2

There are five short conversations here. Listen to the questions carefully, and try to find the correct answer. Both the conversations and the questions will be read twice. (1×5=5 points) 听5个短对话，根据每个问题选择正确答案。对话和问题读两遍。

(　　) 1. What preparations will the man make?
A. Buy food.　　B. Buy water.　　C. Buy food and water.

( ) 2. What might be the relationship between the speakers?

A. Teacher and student.

B. Father and policeman.

C. Father and teacher.

( ) 3. How does the woman go to work?

A. By bus. B. By car. C. By bike.

( ) 4. What does the man's father do now?

A. A worker. B. A technician. C. A tour guide.

( ) 5. How many solutions are mentioned in the conversation?

A. Two. B. Three. C. Four.

Task 3

Lily and Li Wei are talking about sports. Listen carefully and try to find the correct answer for each question. The conversation will be read twice. (2×5=10 points) 莉莉和李伟正在谈论运动。请仔细听对话，并根据对话内容为每个问题选择正确答案。对话读两遍。

( ) 1. Why does Li Wei look so refreshed?

A. Because he is a big fan of soccer.

B. Because he quit playing video games recently and now does sport regularly.

C. Because he is on diet.

( ) 2. What sport does Li Wei do?

A. Basketball. B. Jogging. C. Soccer.

( ) 3. How often does Li Wei do sport?

A. Two or three times a week.

B. Two or three times a month.

C. Three or four times a week.

(　　) 4. Why didn't Lily take part in any sport?

A. Because she is busy with her work.

B. Because she doesn't like doing sport.

C. Because she is busy with her study.

(　　) 5. Li Wei thinks ________ is good for study.

A. getting regular exercise

B. getting regular sleep

C. getting focused

新课标理念下的阅读专项检测范例

（一）

Task 1

You and your classmates are discussing which club to choose. Match the clubs with the pictures. (2×5=10 points) 你和同学们正在讨论选择哪个社团。请将下列社团与对应的图片配对。

A. dancing club	B. painting club	C. English club
D. drama club	E. sports club	

1. ____________

2. ____________

3. ____________

4. ____________

5. ____________

1. ________ 2. ________ 3. ________
4. ________ 5. ________

Task 2

You and your classmates are discussing the special meanings of food from all over the world. Read the following introduction and finish the information card. (2×5=10 points) 你和同学们正讨论世界各国美食的特殊意义。请阅读以下内容，完成信息卡。

Many foods have special meanings. In China, *jiaozi* (dumplings) is one of the main foods during the Chinese New Year. People consider *jiaozi* as a symbol of wealth. In Spain, people eat 12 grapes at midnight on New Year's Eve. Each grape symbolises a lucky month in the coming year. Italians also have a dish that represents wealth and success: green lentils with sausage. Argentinians eat beans on New Year's Day. This stands for keeping the current job or finding a better one in the new year. How interesting these food traditions are! Do you know anything else?

Food with special meanings

Country	Food	Meaning
China	*jiaozi* (dumplings)	1. People consider *jiaozi* as a symbol of 1. ____.
Spain	2. ____	2. Each grape 3. ____ a lucky month in the coming year.
Italy	green lentils with sausage	3. They represent wealth and 4. ____.
Argentina	beans	4. They stand for keeping the current job or finding a 5. ____ one in the new year.

Task 3

You are writing an email to your pen pal Tom to introduce your school day. Complete your email according to the timetable. (1×10=10 points) 你正在给笔友汤姆写邮件，介绍自己一天的校园生活。请根据下面的生活作息表完成邮件。

Time	Activity	Place
6:30	get up	bedroom
7:00	have breakfast	home
7:30	go to school	bus
8:00	attend classes	classroom
12:00	have lunch	dining hall
13:00	do some reading	library
14:00	take skill training classes	workshop
16:00	do sport	school playground
18:00	have dinner	home
19:00	do some housework	home
21:00	go to bed	bedroom

Dear Tom,

I am writing to tell you 1. _______ my school day. I usually 2. _______ at 6:30 in the morning and then 3. _______ breakfast at 7:00. After that, I take a 4. _______ to school 5. _______ have lessons in the classroom. They 6. _______ at 8:00 in the morning and end at 12:00, and then I have lunch 7. _______ the dining hall. I usually do some reading in the library. In the afternoon, I have skill training classes in the 8. _______. They are very interesting. After class, I like doing 9. _______, such as playing basketball with my friends on the school playground. I take the bus 10. _______ home and finish my homework. After dinner, I usually help my mother do some housework. I go to bed at 21:00.

How about your school day? I am looking forward to your reply.

Yours,

Li Ming

Task 4

You are a reporter of the school's radio station. You are preparing an introduction on how people in different countries celebrate the Spring Festival. Help your schoolmates get the key points of the introduction through the following questions. (2×5=10 points) 你是学校广播站的记者，正在准备向校友们介绍世界各地人们庆祝春节的方式。请通过以下问题，帮助校友们提炼下面介绍的要点。

The Spring Festival is celebrated not only in China but also in other parts of the world.

The UK

Celebrations for the Spring Festival in the UK started in 1980, with the first evening party held in 2002. Every Chinese New Year, people get together and have a lot of activities.

The US

The Spring Festival has become a key time for Chinese living or working in the US. They join in a large evening party to welcome the traditional Chinese New Year. It is a good chance for people to build a circle of friends and feel that they are not alone because they share the same culture and value.

Australia

The Chinese New Year is welcomed with three weeks of celebrations across Australia. Many people enjoy fireworks, lion dances, dragon boat races and some other traditional activities.

Singapore

The family dinner on New Year's Eve is an important tradition for Chinese people here. They place traditional food on a table as an act of remembering their past. They usually hold it at home because having it in a restaurant takes away the meaning of the tradition.

(   ) 1. People in ____ began to celebrate the Spring Festival in 1980.

A. the UK　　B. the US　　C. Australia

( ) 2. Why do the Chinese in the US join in a large evening party during the Spring Festival?

A. Because they want to say hello to the Chinese New Year.

B. Because they want to tell others they are alone.

C. Because they want to hold a birthday party for someone.

( ) 3. In Singapore, where do the Chinese families usually hold the New Year dinner?

A. In a restaurant. B. In the countryside. C. At home.

( ) 4. The Chinese New Year is welcomed with ____ weeks of celebrations across Australia.

A. two B. one C. three

( ) 5. Which is TURE according to the introduction?

A. People in Australia like going to the cinema during the Spring Festival.

B. The Spring Festival is celebrated all over the world.

C. The Spring Festival is only celebrated in China.

Task 5

You are the leader of the sports club in Hongxing Vocational School. Now you are talking about the "Trash Running" activity. Answer the following questions according to your introduction. (2×5=10 points) 你是红星职业学校体育社团团长，正在向同学们介绍“捡跑团”活动。请根据介绍的内容，回答下面的问题。

Trash Running

Every Wednesday evening, a group of runners in Chongqing get together and have their 5-to-8-kilometre run in the city. This is not a normal run. The runners take trash (垃圾) bags with them and pick up trash when they run.

"Make running more than just running," Sogor, one of the runners, says. She wears a blue T-shirt with "WE RUN FOR TRASH" on the back. Besides the weekly runs, the group also has family runs once a month. Children and even pets can take part in the activities.

Sogor says there are more than 200 trash runners from all walks of life in the city, such as office workers, yoga teachers and restaurant owners. Over 90 percent of the group members are Chinese. The oldest ones are in their 40s, and the youngest is just five.

"I feel great to make the earth cleaner, " says an 8-year-old boy. He joined the group last month with his parents. The boy broke his left arm, but he kept running and picked up trash with his right hand.

Trash Running came to Shanghai in 2018. There are Trash Running groups in 16 cities like Shanghai, Beijing, Chongqing, Changchun and Wuhan. More than 9,300 runners run and make the cities clean.

(　　) 1. The trash runners run mainly for ________.

A. keeping healthy

B. making the cities clean

C. making more friends

(　　) 2. When do people in Chongqing take part in the "Trash Running" activity?

A. On Mondays.　　B. On Wednesdays.　　C. On Sundays.

(　　) 3. The underlined phrase "all walks of life" means "________" in Chinese.

A. 多才多艺　　B. 各种各样　　C. 各行各业

(　　) 4. What can we learn from the 8-year-old boy?

A. He feels great to make the earth cleaner.

B. He runs with his grandparents.

C. He broke his right hand.

(　　) 5. How many cities have Trash Running groups?

A. 5.　　B. 16.　　C. 40.

（二）

Task 1

You are the chairman of the school's student union, and you are showing the freshmen around the school. Match the school facilities to the pictures. (2×5=10 points) 你是校学生会主席，正在带领新同学熟悉校园环境。请将下列校园设施与对应的图片配对。

A. classroom	B. playground	C. dining hall
D. gym	E. library	

1. ______________

2. ______________

3. ______________

4. ______________

5. ______________

1. ______________ 2. ______________ 3. ______________

4. ______________ 5. ______________

Task 2

You are a waiter/waitress in a restaurant. You are having training about the dishes. Read the passage and complete the form. (2×5=10 points) 你是餐厅的一名服务员，正在接受菜品知识的培训。请阅读以下内容并填写信息卡。

There are different styles of cuisine in China, such as Shandong cuisine, Sichuan cuisine, Guangdong cuisine, Jiangsu cuisine, Fujian cuisine, Hunan cuisine, Anhui cuisine and Zhejiang cuisine. There are four sub-styles in Sichuan cuisine, Chengdu, Chongqing, Zigong and Buddhist vegetarian style. Kung Pao Chicken and Mapo Tofu taste pungent. The hot pot is spicy. Guangdong cuisine tastes clear, light, crisp and fresh. The famous dishes are Sliced Boiled Chicken, Roast Goose and Barbecued Pork in Honey. Jiangsu cuisine is also called Huaiyang cuisine, and it stresses freshness of materials and carving techniques. The most famous dishes are Sweet and Sour Mandarin Fish, Pork Ball and so on.

Cuisine (There are 1. _____ styles of cuisine in China.)		
Style	**Flavour**	**Famous dishes**
Sichuan cuisine	pungent and 2. _____	Kung Pao Chicken, Mapo Tofu and 3. _____
Guangdong cuisine	clear, light, crisp and fresh	Sliced Boiled Chicken, 4. _____ and Barbecued Pork in Honey
Jiangsu cuisine	5. _____ (adj)	Sweet and Sour Mandarin Fish, Pork Ball and so on

Task 3

You are Li Hua, a vocational school student. Your friend Mike just moved to a new place and he feels lonely and has difficulty in making new friends. Complete the letter to him according to the following suggestions. (1×10=10 points) 你是李华，一所职业学校的学生。你的好友迈克搬家后感觉到孤独，不知道如何结交新朋友。请根据下面所给的建议给迈克写一封信。

Suggestions

1. Get out of the house
2. Talk with others
3. Be good at listening
4. Be friendly

Dear Mike,

I'm glad to hear 1. _______ you. I know you feel lonely now and want to make new friends. I will give you some suggestions.

It's hard to make friends 2. _______ you stay at home all the time. Get out of the house and do things that will put you in touch 3. _______ other people. Don't be afraid to show people what you are really good at. Talk 4. _______ the things you like and do best. People will be 5. _______ in you if there is something interesting about you. Look at people in the eye when you talk to them. Be a good 6. _______ (listen). Let people talk about them before talking about yourself. Ask questions, and show 7. _______ interest in their answers. Try to make friends with the kind of people you really like and respect, not just with those who are easy to meet. Be 8. _______ with people. That way, you will have a 9. _______ (big) group of people to choose from and have more chances for 10. _______ friends.

Hope you will make new friends soon.

Yours,

Li Hua

Task 4

You are the manager of a sports club. You've put up a poster for "Walk for Charity". Answer the questions according to the poster. (2×5=10 points) 你是某体育俱乐部的经理，发布了一则"慈善行走"的活动海报。请根据海报内容，回答下列问题。

Walk for Charity (慈善)

Dear friends,

Please join us for "Walk for Charity". Starting from North Street, you and your friends can choose to walk 5, 10, 20 or 30 kilometres.

The money raised will provide support for the rural revitalisation (乡村振兴) of our town. Start getting sponsors (赞助者) now and then simply come along on the day. Please read the instructions below carefully.

See you on Sunday, 28 June.

START TIMES 5km: 8:00 am—11:00 am 10km: 8:00 am—10:30 am 20km: 8:00 am—10:00 am 30km: 8:00 am—9:30 am	**CLOTHING** Clothes should be suitable for the weather. If it is rainy, bring some protections. It is better to wear shoes that have been worn in, rather than new ones.
ROUTE (路线) Maps will be provided at the starting point. If you need help along the route, please tell the volunteers.	**BUSES** A bus will be waiting at Green Street to take walkers back to North Street. The bus will leave every 20 minutes starting from 11:40 am. The service is free.

( ) 1. When will "Walk for Charity" be held?

A. On 28 June. B. On 29 June. C. On 28 July.

( ) 2. As for clothing, the walkers had better wear ________.

A. warm clothes B. cool suits C. old shoes

( ) 3. Li Ming chooses to walk 10 kilometres, when should he start the walk?

A. Before 11:00 am. B. Before 10:30 am. C. Before 10:00 am.

( ) 4. How much does the bus service cost?

A. 10 *yuan*. B. 20 *yuan*. C. Free.

(　　) 5. Which of the following is TRUE?

A. The walkers can get some help while walking.

B. The money raised will be used to build two city libraries.

C. A bus will be waiting at North Street to take the walkers back to Green Street.

Task 5

You are a member of the science club in Hongqi Vocational School. You are introducing three interesting inventions to your classmates. Answer their questions according to the following introduction. (2×5=10 points) 你是红旗职业学校科学社团成员。你在向同学们介绍三种有趣的发明。请根据介绍的内容，回答同学们的提问。

Can you imagine that gloves could talk? Do you want to know what it feels like to fly like a bird? We have picked out three interesting inventions to share with you.

Talking Gloves

Four foreign students have created a pair of gloves, which helps people to communicate with those who have hearing and speaking problems. There are sensors (传感器) on the gloves. They recognise (辨认出) sign language and translate it into text on a smartphone. Then the smartphone changes the text to spoken words. In this way, people can understand sign language easily.

Google Glasses

Google Glasses are like a computer built into a pair of glasses. The glasses allow you to surf the Internet and make calls without even lifting a finger. The glasses also have a camera and a GPS mapping system. Users can take and share photos, check maps and surf the Internet just by moving their eyeballs.

Wingsuits

The suit realises your dream of flying like a bird, well, not exactly flying, but gliding (滑翔) through the air. It increases the surface area of the human body, which makes it easier for people to float (漂浮) in the air. Fliers wearing Wingsuits can glide one kilometre in about 30 seconds.

(　　) 1. What inventions are introduced?

A. Talking Gloves; Google Glasses; Wingsuits.

B. Smiling Gloves; Google Watches; Wingsuits.

C. Talking Gloves; Google Glasses; Swimsuits.

(　　) 2. What do Talking Gloves help people understand?

A. Spoken words.

B. Sign language.

C. The text on the smartphone.

(　　) 3. How can users of Google Glasses surf the Internet?

A. By speaking to the glasses.

B. By lifting a finger.

C. By moving their eyeballs.

(　　) 4. What can fliers do if they wear Wingsuits?

A. They can check maps.

B. They can glide through the air.

C. They can take and share photos.

(　　) 5. Which statement is TRUE according to introductions?

A. Talking Gloves are made for people who have hearing and speaking problems.

B. Google Glasses are sensors built into a pair of glasses.

C. You can fly like a bird if you wear the Wingsuit.

新课标理念下的写作专项检测范例

(一)

Task

You are Li Hua, a new student in a vocational school. You want to introduce your major to your American friend David. Write a letter according to the following information. (10 points) 你是李华，一所职业学校的新生，想跟你的美国朋友戴维介绍你所学的专业。请根据下表内容给他写封信。

An introduction about my major	
Major	Secretary
Main subjects	history, art, oral practice, public relations
Skills needed	◆ Mandarin ◆ English ◆ communication skills
Future jobs	secretary, assistant

Dear David,

Long time no see. How is it going? I am studying at a vocational school now.

____

____

____

____.

I am looking forward to hearing from you!

Yours,

Li Hua

（二）

Task

You are a member of the school's cookery club. Write a notice about the activity to be held in your club according to the following information. (10 points) 你是学校烹饪社团的成员。请根据以下信息为社团即将举行的活动写一份通知。

Theme of the activity	Food and memory
Activity	share your stories about food
Time	25 January
Place	Happy Café
How to join	log on to the club's official website

Notice

____

____

____

____

____.

The Cookery Club

20 January 2024

三 探索落实学科核心素养及体现课程育人价值的综合检测任务示例

基于学科核心素养的综合检测任务

（一）

Speaking （Task 1–Task 3，共20分）

Task 1

You and William are good friends. You're talking about school clubs. Read the names of the clubs loudly. (0.5×10=5 points) 你和威廉是好朋友。你们正在谈论学校的社团。请大声读出以下社团的名字。

1. football club
2. basketball club
3. dancing club
4. English club
5. photography club
6. singing club
7. art club
8. guitar club
9. *hanfu* club
10. street dance club

Task 2

You are Li Hua, a waiter in a restaurant. Now you're receiving a guest. Read the conversation loudly. (5 points) 你是李华，是某饭店的服务员。现在你正在接待一位客人。请大声读出以下对话。

Li Hua: Good evening! A table for two?

Guest: Yes. I'd like a table by the window.

Li Hua: No problem. This way please, sir.

Guest: I'd like to have the menu, please.

Li Hua: Here you are. Take your time.

Guest: Thank you!

Task 3

Li Hua is a vocational school student. He is talking about the school club he wants to join. Read the following introduction loudly. (10 points) 李华是一所职业学校的学生，正在谈论他想加入的社团。请大声读出以下内容。

> My favourite subject is English. My English teacher, Ms. Wang, teaches us very well. She always tries to design many interesting activities in her class, which can draw our interest in English learning. And she spends a lot of time with us. Many students improve their English very quickly. So do I. But I'm a little bit shy, so I'm afraid to speak English in front of people. Ms. Wang encourages me to join the English club, because it is useful and fun. Besides, as an E-commerce major, I'm sure that good English will help me a lot in my future job. So now I am a member of the English club.

Listening （Task 4–Task 6，共20分）

Task 4

You are a student from Xinhua Vocational School. Now you are talking about your relationship with your classmate, Grace. You are going to hear five questions. Listen carefully and respond. Each question will be read twice. (1×5=5 points) 你是新华职业学校的一名学生。你正在谈论你和同学格雷丝的关系。你将听到5个问题。请听提问并做出回应。每个问题读两遍。

(　　) 1. A. We met at the basketball club and had lots to talk about.
B. She is one of my close friends.
C. Friendship is important.

(　　) 2. A. I knew Grace well.
B. She is good at solving problems.
C. I get along well with Grace. We enjoy spending time together.

(　　) 3. A. Understand and respect each other.
B. Both of us are fond of reading.
C. We have many things in common.

(　　) 4. A. She likes watching films.
B. She is helpful and open-minded.
C. She makes an apology to me.

(　　) 5. A. They make you feel valued and loved.
B. They have the same hobbies.
C. Staying alone all the time.

Task 5

There are five short conversations here. Listen to the questions carefully, and try to find the correct answer. Both the conversations and the questions will be read twice. (1×5=5 points) 听5个短对话，根据每个问题选择正确答案。对话和问题读两遍。

(　　) 1. What is the man's plan for this weekend?
A. Going shopping.
B. Visiting some old friends.
C. Staying at home.

(　　) 2. What activity do people in Thailand have in the New Year?
A. It's great fun.
B. Everyone enjoys it.
C. Splash water on each other.

(　　) 3. What are they talking about?
A. Food.　　B. Weather.　　C. People.

(　　) 4. What natural disaster do we know from the conversation?
A. A typhoon.　　B. An earthquake.　　C. A sandstorm.

(　　) 5. What are they talking about?
A. Doing some cleaning.
B. Sorting refuse.
C. Picking up the rubbish.

Task 6

You are Li Mei who is new in a vocational school. You are asking Lin Tao the way on campus. Listen carefully and try to find the correct answer for each question. The conversation will be read twice. (2×5=10 points) 你是李梅，刚到一所职业学校。你正在向林涛问路。请仔细听对话，并根据对话内容为每个问题选择正确答案。对话读两遍。

(   ) 1. Where is Li Mei going?
A. The library. B. The dining hall. C. The supermarket.

(   ) 2. Where is the dining hall?
A. Opposite the library.
B. In the library.
C. On the first floor.

(   ) 3. How can Li Mei get to the dining hall?
A. Turn right.
B. Go straight along the road and turn left.
C. Keep walking for five minutes.

(   ) 4. Did Li Mei know the way to the dining hall?
A. No, she didn't.
B. Yes, she was familiar with the school.
C. She was not sure.

(   ) 5. How far is it to the dining hall?
A. A long way. B. Three kilometres. C. It's about three minutes' walk.

Reading （Task 7–Task 11，共50分）

Task 7

You are a student studying at a vocational school. In a class meeting, you and your classmates are talking about careers which you can choose from after graduating from school. Match the jobs to the pictures. (2×5=10 points) 你是一名职业学校在校生，在班会课上，你和同学们正在讨论毕业后可以选择的职业。请将下列职业与对应的图片配对。

A. chef	B. shop assistant	C. waitress
D. secretary	E. tour guide	

1. ______________

2. ______________

3. ______________

4. ______________

5. ______________

1. ______________ 2. ______________ 3. ______________

4. ______________ 5. ______________

Task 8

You are a tour guide of a travel agency. You are trying to find some information about the weather and preparing for travelling. Read the weather report and complete the form. (2×5=10 points) 你是旅行社的一名导游，正在查询近期的天气预报，为出团做准备。请阅读下面的天气预报，填写表格。

Good morning! Here's the weather report for some cities. It's going to snow with the highest temperature of 5°C below zero in Harbin today. Please keep warm when going out. Our capital city will be sunny with a strong wind, with the highest temperature of 9°C and the lowest of 5°C. It's cold, so remember to wear warm clothes when going out. Nanning is sunny with a temperature from 15°C to 20°C. In Guiyang, the temperature ranges from 8°C to 13°C. It's cloudy in the morning and rainy in the evening. People should wear more clothes at night in case of catching a cold. Chongqing is rainy in the daytime and has a strong wind during the night with a temperature from 11°C to 15°C. There will be beautiful sunshine in Haikou. People will feel comfortable to go out as the temperature is from 20°C to 26°C. That's the weather report for today.

City	Weather	The highest temperature	The lowest temperature	Remark
Harbin	snow	1. _____°C	/	keep warm
2. _____	sunny, windy	9°C	5°C	wear warm clothes
Nanning	sunny	20°C	15°C	/
Guiyang	cloudy to 3. _____	13°C	8°C	4. _____ at night
Chongqing	rainy, windy	15°C	11°C	/
Haikou	5. _____	26°C	20°C	feel comfortable

Task 9

You are Li Hua, the monitor of your class. You'd like to invite the teachers to attend your Mid-Autumn Festival party. Complete the invitation letter according to the following information. (1×10=10 points) 你是班长李华，想要邀请老师们参加中秋节聚会。请根据下面的信息完成邀请信。

Dear teachers,

Our class 1. _______ (be) going to hold 2. _______ interesting party for the Mid-Autumn Festival 3. _______ 12 October. We would like 4. _______ (invite) you to the party.

The party will start in the school hall 5. _______ seven o'clock in the evening. It will be very interesting. You can enjoy 6. _______ (sing) festival songs. What's more, there will 7. _______ (be) traditional Chinese art shows, including calligraphy and paper cutting. At last, we will have mooncakes and play interesting games to win prizes 8. _______ (happy). I'm sure you will be 9. _______ (interest) in it. If you'd like to join us, please let me know.

Looking forward to 10. _______ (see) you at the party.

Yours sincerely,

Li Hua

Task 10

You are Wang Li. You are going to share some tips on how to build friendships. Answer the questions according to what you are going to talk about. (2×5=10 points) 你是王莉，准备与同学们分享朋友相处的原则。请根据你准备的内容，回答同学们的问题。

Hi, I'm Wang Li. My best friend is Wu Lin. We have been close friends for over five years. Both of us are fond of reading. We often read the same book and discuss it together. We both think that reading can not only enrich our knowledge but also help us make new friends. We have many things in common and enjoy spending time together. But this doesn't mean that we never quarrel with each other. Whether in good times or bad times, we always follow three rules: understand and respect each other; avoid arguments and difficult topics; keep in touch and pay attention to small details. These rules work effectively for us to get along well. Do you have your own friendship rules? If so, what are they?

(   ) 1. How long have you and Wu Lin been close friends?

A. Over 5 years.   B. Less than 5 years.   C. Over 3 years.

(　　) 2. What are you and Wu Lin fond of?

A. Jogging.　　B. Reading.　　C. Hiking.

(　　) 3. Did you and Wu Lin ever quarrel with each other?

A. No, never.　　B. Yes, sometimes.　　C. Not mentioned.

(　　) 4. How many rules do you and Wu Lin follow to build your friendship?

A. Three.　　B. Four.　　C. Five.

(　　) 5. Which rule do you and Wu Lin follow in terms of friendship?

A. Understand and respect each other.

B. Welcome arguments and difficult topics.

C. Pay no attention to small details.

Task 11

You are Li Hua and you are introducing the Dragon Boat Festival to foreign friends. Help your foreign friends to complete the information card according to your introduction. (2×5=10 points) 你是李华，正在向外国朋友介绍端午节。请根据介绍的内容，帮助外国朋友填写信息表。

The Dragon Boat Festival, which falls on the fifth day of the fifth lunar month, is one of the traditional Chinese festivals. The Dragon Boat Festival has many origins. One of them is to honour Qu Yuan, an ancient Chinese poet. *Zongzi* is a traditional Chinese food eaten during the Dragon Boat Festival. The most popular activity during the Dragon Boat Festival is the dragon boat race. It is exciting and interesting, and it has now become an international sport.

The Dragon Boat Festival	
Time	It falls on the 1. ___________ day of the fifth lunar month.
Origin	One of them is to honour an ancient Chinese poet, 2. ___________.

Food	3. ________ is a traditional Chinese food eaten during the Dragon Boat Festival.
Activity	The most 4. ________ activity during the Dragon Boat Festival is the dragon boat race, which has now become an international 5. ________.

Writing （Task 12，共10分）

Task 12

You are a student from Bright Vocational School. You are talking about your favourite teacher. Write a brief introduction according to the following information. (15 points) 你是光明职业学校的一名学生，正在谈论你最喜欢的老师。请根据以下信息介绍你的老师。

My favourite teacher

Name	Miss Li
Age	about 30 years old
Subject	Chinese
Her classes	interesting and relaxing
Character	patient and easy-going
Hobbies	◆ singing and dancing ◆ reading books

My favourite teacher

Hello, everyone. Here I'm glad to introduce my favourite teacher. ________

____

____

____

____

（二）

Speaking（Task 1–Task 3，共20分）

Task 1

You're Li Hua. You and Zhang Li are vocational school students. You are talking about the subjects offered by vocational schools. Read the subjects loudly. (0.5×10=5 points) 你是李华，你和张莉都是职业学校学生。你们正在谈论职业学校开设的课程。请大声将这些课程读出来。

1. Chinese
2. nursing
3. history
4. English
5. chemistry
6. programme design
7. mechanical basics
8. cookery
9. music
10. P.E.

Task 2

You are Li Hua. You and Yan Hong are talking about your close friends. Read the conversation loudly and share it with us. (5 points) 你是李华，正跟严红谈论你们的好朋友。请大声读出对话跟我们分享。

Yan Hong: Could you tell me something about your close friend, Zhao Bin?

Li Hua: Sure. We met in the basketball club.

Yan Hong: Oh, I see. So both of you are fond of playing basketball.

Li Hua: That's right. Who is your best friend?

Yan Hong: Li Wei. We both like taking photos outdoors.

Li Hua: It feels good to have friends.

Task 3

Li Hua is introducing traditional Chinese food to foreign friends. Read the following introduction loudly. (10 points) 李华正在向外国友人介绍中国的传统美食。请大声朗读下文。

We all need food to live. In fact, many foods have special meanings. All around the world, food plays an important part in a country's culture. For example, in China, we have *jiaozi*, which is one of the main foods during the Spring Festival. It's a traditional Chinese food. Ancient people considered *jiaozi* as a symbol of wealth because it looked like an ancient coin, Yuanbao. Now Chinese people give it a new meaning. Whenever the family get together, people will eat *jiaozi*, which represents being together as a family.

Listening （Task 4–Task 6，共20分）

Task 4

You are ordering food at a restaurant. You are going to hear five questions from the waiter. Listen carefully and respond. Each question will be read twice. (1×5=5 points) 你正在餐馆点餐。你将听到服务员的5个问题。请听提问并做出回应。每个问题读两遍。

(　　) 1. A. Yes, please.
B. No, no smoking here.
C. Yes, a table for two.

(　　) 2. A. I'd like the mushroom soup to start with.
B. I'd like the tomato soup, fruit salad and a steak.
C. It's too spicy.

(　　) 3. A. Orange juice, please.
B. A steak, please.
C. Fruit salad, please.

(　　) 4. A. Medium, please.
B. Sweet, please.
C. Rice, please.

(　　) 5. A. A tomato, please.
B. A burger, please.
C. A large soda, please.

Task 5

There are five short conversations here. Listen to the question carefully, and try to find the correct answer. Both the conversations and questions will be read twice. (1×5=5 points) 听5个短对话，根据每个问题选择正确答案。对话和问题读两遍。

(　　) 1. Which city is the man from?
A. France.　　B. Paris.　　C. Beijing.

(　　) 2. How long will it take by bus?
A. Half an hour.
B. More than half an hour.
C. Less than half an hour.

(　　) 3. Which is not mentioned in the conversation?
A. Buy food and water.
B. Check medical supplies.
C. Move the flowerpots off the balcony.

(　　) 4. Which festival are they talking about?
A. The Spring Festival.
B. The Mid-Autumn Festival.
C. The Lantern Festival.

(　　) 5. What kind of school is the man probably in?
A. A general school.
B. A vocational school.
C. A primary school.

Task 6

Joe is asking the way and Wu Lin is answering now. Listen carefully and try to find the correct answer for each question. The conversation will be read twice. (2×5=10 points) 乔正在向吴琳问路。请仔细听对话，并根据对话内容为每个问题选择正确答案。对话读两遍。

( ) 1. Where does Joe want to go?

A. Next block. B. Hongya Cave. C. Next street.

( ) 2. Where is Hongya Cave?

A. On the riverside. B. By a park. C. On a rock.

( ) 3. How can Joe go to Hongya Cave?

A. On foot. B. By car. C. By subway.

( ) 4. How far is Hongya Cave from Joe?

A. Ten minutes' walk.

B. Five minutes' walk.

C. Ten minutes' drive.

( ) 5. There are not only many interesting places but also _______ here.

A. the park B. Chongqing-style life C. the scenery

Reading (Task 7–Task 11，共50分)

Task 7

Do you have interest in the following careers? Match the pictures with them. (2×5=10 points) 你对下面的职业感兴趣吗？请将下列职业与对应的图片配对。

A. vocational school teacher	B. air hostess
C. nurse	D. computer programmer
E. auto repair worker	

1. ______________ 2. ______________ 3. ______________

4. ______________ 5. ______________

1. ______________ 2. ______________ 3. ______________
4. ______________ 5. ______________

Task 8

You are a vocational school student. You are going to introduce your school life to your family. Complete the information card according to your introduction. (2×5=10 points) 你是职业学校的一名学生，准备向家人介绍你的校园生活。请根据你准备的介绍，完成信息卡。

Do you want to know about my vocational school? Let me tell you. We learn English, Chinese, history, etc. in the classroom, and have skill-training classes in workshops. Our teachers always give us lots of practical tips. They are very helpful. The skill-training teachers come from different fields. Some are workers in factories or chefs in restaurants, others are tour guides from travel agencies or secretaries working for companies... All of our teachers are not only knowledgeable and experienced, but also very kind and friendly. I'm sure I'll learn a lot from them.

I'm really happy at this new school.

My vocational school	
School	Do you want to know about my 1. _____ school?
Subjects	We learn English, Chinese, history, etc. in the classroom, and have skill-training classes in 2. _____.
Teachers	All of our teachers are not only knowledgeable and experienced, but also very 3. _____ and 4. _____.
Feeling	I'm really 5. _____ at this new school.

Task 9

The school clubs are recruiting new students. Complete the poster according to the given information. (1×10=10 points) 学校社团正在火热招新中。请根据所给信息完成招新海报。

Club name	Activities	Time	Location	Participants (招生对象)
Music club	learn music knowledge, play instruments, participate in concerts and performances	every Wednesday from 3:00 pm to 5:00 pm	in the music classroom	students interested in music
Sports club	play basketball, football, badminton, etc.	every Friday from 4:00 pm to 6:00 pm	at the gym	students interested in sports
English club	practise English skills, take part in English dramas	every Thursday from 4:00 pm to 6:00 pm	in the library	students interested in English

The school clubs have started to register new members. 1. ________ one do you like to join?

If you are interested 2. ________ music, please join the music club. You can learn music knowledge, 3. ________ instruments, and take part in concerts and performances. You are welcome on every Wednesday from 3:00 pm to 5:00 pm in the music classroom.

4. ________ you are interested in sports, the sports club is your best 5. ________. You may play all kinds of sports 6. ________ basketball, football, and badminton. Come every Friday from 4:00 pm to 6:00 pm at the school gym.

If you want to learn English 7. ________, come to the English club. Here you can improve English listening, speaking, reading, and 8. ________ skills, as well as take part in English dramas. We will 9. ________ for you every Thursday from 4:00 pm to 6:00 pm in the school library.

Join a club, and you will learn more and 10. ________ more friends.

Task 10

You are a reporter of Hongxing Vocational School. You are introducing the festivals about the moon around the world. Answer the questions according to your introduction. (2×5=10 points) 你是红星职业学校的记者，正在向同学们介绍关于月亮的中外节日。请根据介绍回答下列问题。

People in Asia love the moon. They have festivals when the moon is full.

In China, people celebrate the Mid-Autumn Festival. It is a big holiday. People have dinner parties. They eat mooncakes. They admire the full moon.

Vietnam celebrates the moon, too. The holiday is called "Tết Trung Thu". It has a story about a man. His name is Cuội. He hung on to a banyan (菩提) tree. The tree floated up to the moon.

In Sri Lanka, every full moon day is a public holiday. They are called Poya

Days. They happen around 12 times a year. People go to temples on these days. They dance and sing.

In Myanmar, Thadingyut is the second most popular holiday. It is a festival of lights. It is held on the full moon of the Burmese lunar month of Thadingyut.

(　　) 1. Which country celebrates a festival when the moon is full besides China?

A. the US.　　B. Vietnam.　　C. France.

(　　) 2. What do people do during the Mid-Autumn Festival in China?

A. They eat mooncakes.

B. They admire the full moon.

C. Both A and B.

(　　) 3. What is the moon festival called in Vietnam?

A. Poya Days.　　B. Tết Trung Thu.　　C. Thadingyut.

(　　) 4. In Sri Lanka, the full moon days happen around ______ times a year.

A. 8　　B. 10　　C. 12

(　　) 5. In Myanmar, the second most popular holiday is called a festival of ______.

A. flowers　　B. lights　　C. songs

Task 11

You are the leader of the P.E. department in Hongxing Vocational School. You're making a survey about teens' sleep. Answer the following questions and introduce your survey. (2×5=10 points) 你是红星职业学校学生会体育部部长。你对青少年睡眠质量做了调查。请回答以下问题，向同学们汇报调查情况。

Teens' sleep survey

9–10 hours' sleep is what most teens need a night. However, the study shows as follows:

60% of teens sleep for about 7 hours at night.	21% of teens find it difficult to fall asleep.	56% of teens feel tired sometimes while 24% feel tired all the time.

What may keep teens awake at night?

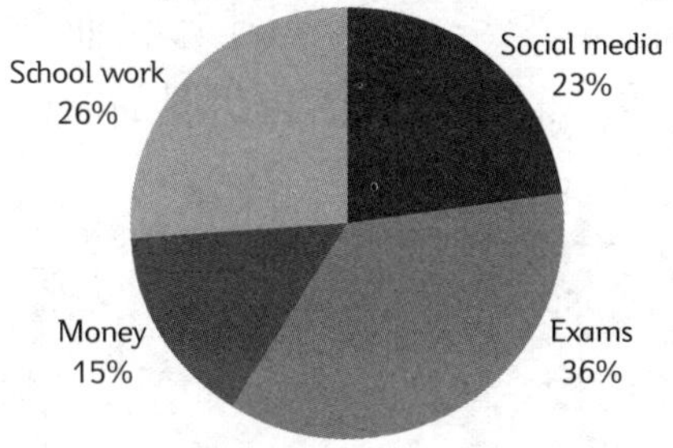

How do teens get to sleep?

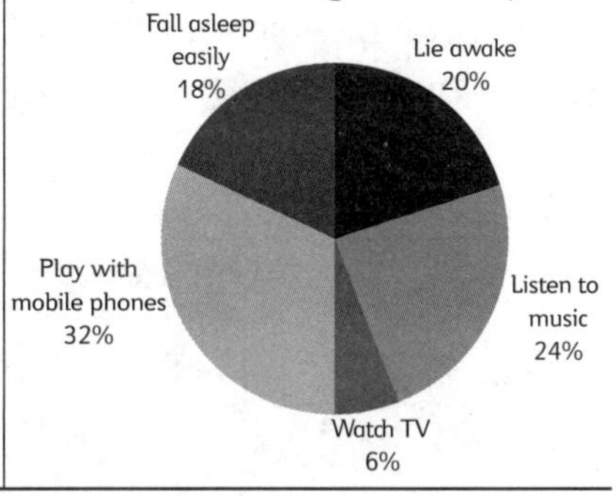

( ) 1. Most teens need ______ hours' sleep a night.

A. 7–8 B. 8–9 C. 9–10

( ) 2. According to the survey, ______ of teens find it difficult to fall asleep.

A. 60% B. 21% C. 56%

( ) 3. ______ has/have the greatest effect to keep teens awake at night.

A. Social media B. Exams C. School work

( ) 4. Most of teens get to sleep by ______.

A. listening to music

B. watching TV

C. playing with mobile phones

( ) 5. According to the survey, we can know that ________.

A. 60% of teens sleep for about 8 hours at night

B. 24% of teens feel tired sometimes

C. it's important for teens to have enough sleep

Writing （Task 12，共10分）

Task 12

You are Li Hua, a new student from a vocational school. You want to share your new school life with your American friend, David. Write a letter to tell him about your new school life. (10 points) 你是李华，一名刚上职业学校的学生，想和美国朋友戴维分享你的校园生活。请写一封信告诉他你的近况。

An introduction about the vocational school life	
Major	Computer Science
What to learn	English, Chinese, history and practical skills
Where to learn	◆ in the classroom ◆ in workshops
Club activities	dancing club
Want to know	David's study and life

Dear David,

Long time no see. How is everything going? I am studying at a vocational school. ____

____

____

____

____.

I am looking forward to hearing from you!

Yours,

Li Hua

（三）

Speaking （Task 1–Task 3，共20分）

Task 1

You're Li Hua. You and Zhang Li are both vocational school students. You are talking about the diversity of modern transportation modes. Read the transportation modes loudly. (0.5×10=5 points) 你是李华。你和张莉都是职业学校学生。你们正在谈论现代交通工具的多样性。请大声将交通工具读出来。

1. bus
2. shared bike
3. high-speed train
4. subway
5. plane
6. ferry
7. ship
8. boat
9. car
10. regular train

Task 2

You are Li Hua, a reporter of the school radio. Now you're interviewing students on campus. Read the conversation loudly. (5 points) 你是校园电台的记者李华。现在你正在校园采访同学。请大声读出以下对话。

Li Hua: Excuse me. Would you please tell me your favourite festival?

Student A: Sure. My favourite festival is the Spring Festival.

Li Hua: Why do you like it so much?

Student A: Because it is the most important traditional Chinese festival.

Li Hua: I agree with you. Thank you very much.

Student A: You're welcome.

Task 3

Li Lan and Zhou Li are in the same class, and they are good friends. But today, Li Lan is a little upset. She has quarreled with Zhou Li. Read the following passage to see what really happened to them. (10 points) 李兰和周丽是同班同学，还是好朋友。但是今天李兰不太开心。她跟周丽发生了争吵。请大声读出下列文章，看看她们到底怎么了。

Li Lan looks a bit down today. It seems something is bothering her. One of her close friends, Zhou Li, got angry with her. What on earth happened? It turns out that Li Lan was worried about the final exams and under great pressure. She shouted at Zhou Li over a small issue yesterday. Zhou Li left in anger and refused to talk to Li Lan. Li Lan decides to make an apology to Zhou Li first and wants to get her forgiveness. As a good friend, she should be more patient and considerate. Whether in good times or bad times, friends should understand and respect each other.

Listening （Task 4–Task 6，共20分）

Task 4

Lily and Zhou Bo are talking about Zhou Bo's new school. You are going to hear five questions. Listen carefully and respond. Each question will be read twice. (1×5=5 points) 莉莉和周博正在谈论周博的新学校。你将听到5个问题。请听提问并做出回应。每个问题读两遍。

(　　) 1. A. Very good.　　B. Like what?　　C. Not very.

(　　) 2. A. We have skill-training workshops.
B. In no way.
C. It's very good.

(　　) 3. A. I like it a lot.
B. We can play basketball.
C. We can learn how to operate different machines.

(　　) 4. A. Friends.　　B. Mechanical basics.　　C. Noodles.

(　　) 5. A. Because I like it.
B. Because it's interesting and useful.
C. Because I am the best.

Task 5

There are five short conversations here. Listen to the questions carefully, and try to find the correct answer. Both the conversations and the questions will be read twice. (1×5=5 points) 听5个短对话，根据每个问题选择正确答案。对话和问题读两遍。

( ) 1. How much is the T-shirt?
A. $19.15. B. $9.15. C. $9.18.

( ) 2. Will Jane go camping this weekend?
A. Yes. B. No. C. Not sure.

( ) 3. Where does the conversation probably take place?
A. At a school. B. In a hospital. C. In a restaurant.

( ) 4. What is the weather like now?
A. Warm. B. Cloudy. C. Rainy.

( ) 5. What does Lynn do now?
A. He is doing e-commerce.
B. He is a shop assistant.
C. He is a singer.

Task 6

Joe is calling Jane about their appointment. Listen carefully and try to find the correct answer for each question. The conversation will be read twice. (2×5=10 points) 乔正在就他们约定见面的事，给简打电话。请仔细听对话，并根据对话内容为每个问题选择正确答案。对话读两遍。

( ) 1. Why does Joe call Jane?
A. To say that he'll be late.
B. To invite her to dinner.
C. To tell her about his work.

( ) 2. Why is Joe late?

A. Because the film begins late.

B. Because he has to finish a report first.

C. Because he ate something.

( ) 3. What will Joe and Jane probably do tonight?

A. Have dinner together.

B. See a film together.

C. Work together.

( ) 4. When is Joe going to see Jane?

A. 6:00. B. 6:15. C. 6:45.

( ) 5. What does Joe suggest Jane do before he arrives?

A. Have something to eat. B. See a film.

C. Do some work.

Reading (Task 7–Task 11，共50分)

Task 7

You and your friends are talking about your favourite sports. Match the sports with the pictures. (2×5=10 points) 你和朋友们正在谈论喜欢的运动。请将下列运动与对应的图片配对。

A. doing Taichi	B. playing basketball	C. doing sit-ups
D. rock-climbing	E. jogging	

1. ________________

2. ________________

3. ________________

4. ________

5. ________

1. ________ 2. ________ 3. ________
4. ________ 5. ________

Task 8

You are a member of Green Club in the school. You and your partners are preparing some theme activities for the creation of a green school. Read the activities and finish the information card. (2×5=10 points) 你是学校环保俱乐部的一员。你和伙伴们正在筹备一些主题活动，号召大家共建绿色校园。阅读活动内容，完成信息卡。

There will be some activities for creating a green school next Friday afternoon. Welcome to join us. We need to make some changes in our daily habits. First, let's remember to turn off lights and electronic devices when they are not in use. Second, we should save water by taking shorter showers and fixing any leaks (漏水) promptly. Third, we must recycle and properly sort garbage. Fourth, we can plant more trees and flowers around the school to enhance the natural beauty of our campus.

I believe that if we work together, we can make a significant difference in protecting our planet. Let's take the initiative and start from our school.

Creating a green school	
Theme	There will be some activities for creating a 1. _____ school.

What to do	We need to make some 2. _____ in our daily habits.
How to do	First, remember to turn off lights 3. _____ they are not in use. 4. _____ , save water. Third, recycle and properly sort garbage. Fourth, plant 5. _____ trees and flowers.

Task 9

You are the editor of your school newspaper. You are preparing a report on an Olympic champion. Complete the task according to the following information. (1×10=10 points) 你是校报编辑，正在准备一期奥运冠军的报道。请根据下列信息完成报道内容。

The Olympic champion—Quan Hongchan

Name	Quan Hongchan
Nationality	Chinese
Place of birth	Zhanjiang, Guangdong province
Date of birth	28 March 2007
Known for	diving of women's 10m platform
Achievements	gold medal winner of the 2020 World Aquatics Championships, and the 2020 Tokyo Olympic Games

Quan Hongchan is a Chinese diver 1. _________ was born in Zhanjiang, Guangdong province 2. _________ 28 March 2007. She won the gold medal in the 3. _________ 10m platform event at the 2020 Tokyo Olympics, 4. _________ her the first Chinese diver to win two Olympic gold 5. _________ in this event. Quan started diving at the 6. _________ of six and has won numerous awards and championships, including the 2020 World Aquatics Championships and the 2020 Tokyo Olympic Games. She is 7. _________ for her exceptional technical skills and her ability 8. _________ perform 9. _________ pressure. Quan is considered one of the top 10. _________ in the world.

Task 10

You're a student of Hongxing Vocational School. You think a timetable can help students be organised. Now you are sharing your plan for next week and answering questions. (2×5=10 points) 你是红星职业学校的学生。你认为计划表能帮助大家变得更有条理。现在你正与大家分享你下周的计划并回答以下问题。

My plan for next week	
Monday	study group meeting at 3:00 pm
Tuesday	basketball match at 4:30 pm
Wednesday	seeing some friends at 2:00 pm
Thursday	art class from 7:30 pm to 8:30 pm
Friday	volunteer (志愿者) work at the student centre from 2:00 pm to 4:00 pm
Saturday	shopping at 10:00 am
Sunday	basketball team party at 8:00 pm

(　　) 1. I'm going to take part in a basketball match on ________.
A. Monday evening　B. Tuesday afternoon　C. Friday morning

(　　) 2. On Wednesday afternoon I'm going to ________.
A. enjoy the concert　B. see some friends　C. see a doctor

(　　) 3. The art class will last for ________.
A. an hour　B. one hour and a half　C. two hours

(　　) 4. I will do the volunteer work ________.
A. on the playground　B. in the classroom　C. at the student centre

(　　) 5. My basketball team party starts at ________on Sunday.
A. 7:30 pm　B. 8:00 pm　C. 8:30 pm

Task 11

You're a member of the school's science club. Introduce VR technology to students and answer questions. (2×5=10 points) 你是学校科学社团的成员。请向同学们介绍虚拟现实技术，并回答下列问题。

> What is virtual reality? It's an artificial world made by a computer. How do users experience it? They wear a VR headset. It blocks out sights of the real world. Then, users see a simulated world. It seems to have depth. The users feel as if they were inside the 3-D space.
>
> How does VR help people? It can make video games seem more real. It can also help relieve (缓解) pain. Facing fears in VR can help people conquer (克服) those fears in real life. It can also help bring history to life.
>
> With the new technology, people who can't hold hand controllers could control the virtual reality with facial expressions.

( ) 1. Virtual reality is an artificial world made by ________.

A. a head　　B. a machine　　C. a computer

( ) 2. How does a user experience the artificial world?

A. By wearing a pair of glasses.

B. By wearing a VR headset.

C. By closing the eyes.

( ) 3. What will happen if a user wears a VR headset?

A. The user will see a real world.

B. The user will feel as if he or she were inside the 4-D space.

C. The VR headset will block out sights of the real world.

( ) 4. How does VR help people?

A. It can make video games become real.

B. It can help stop the pain.

C. It can help bring history to life.

(　　) 5. With the new technology, people could control the virtual reality with________.

A. hand controllers　　B. 3-D space　　C. facial expressions

Writing （Task 12，共10分）

Task 12

You are a reporter of the school's radio station. You have asked 100 students how they go to school. Write an interview report. (10 points) 你是学校广播站的记者。为了解同学们上学的交通方式，你采访了100名学生。请写一份采访报告。

Students

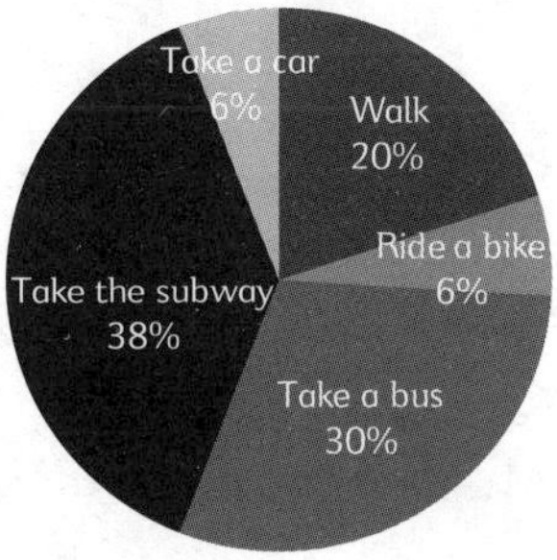

How do you go to school?

Different students have different ways to go to school. Here is the survey.

____

____

____

____

____

高二篇

四 基于学科核心素养培养的中职英语教学评价检测解析

《中等职业学校英语课程标准（2020年版）》（以下简称《课程标准》）明确指出：评价应以促进学科核心素养的养成为目标，构建课程、教学、评价相统一的评价体系。评价要关注学生职场语言沟通、思维差异感知、跨文化理解和自主学习等学科核心素养的发展，应能全面反映学生英语学科核心素养的发展状况和应达到的水平。

高二的中职英语教学评价检测基于这个学段的国规教材及教学实际，聚焦英语课程目标，充分考虑英语学科核心素养培养的综合性和生成性，探索基于真实情境和现实意义的表现性评价，检测学生在学习后是否获得了相应的职场语言沟通、思维差异感知、跨文化理解和自主学习等核心素养，力争使评价从知识本位转向关注学生全面发展，考查学生英语学科核心素养的发展状况，同时关注课程思政及英语学科的人文性和课程育人价值。

中职英语教学评价检测，通过创设生动真实的生活或职业情境，引导学生运用所学知识进行语言理解、语言表达和语言交互，让学生运用在英语教学中发展起来的职场语言沟通能力、思维差异感知能力、跨文化理解能力和自主学习能力去完成生活或职场任务，从而全面落实立德树人的根本任务。该检测由听、说、读、写四部分共12个任务构成，包含《课程标准》要求的"人与自我""人与自然"、"人与社会"三大主题范围，涉及饮食起居，校园生活，个人、家庭及社区生活，出行问路，体育运动，自然环境，灾害防范，环境保护，历史人物与事件，庆典、聚会等话题。"说"是语言应用、与人开口沟通的第一步，对应"职场语言沟通"素养。我们把"说"放在第一部分，从Task 1到Task 3，要求学生朗读词汇、对话和短文，内容包括谈论伟大发明、酒店日常工作和时间管理。第二部分是"听"，从Task 4到Task 6，从听句子到短对话和长对话，内容包括个人生活、购物和就医。需要注意的是，与注重初中阶段衔接的高一听力检测不同，高二Task 5更加注重情境的完整性，增加了听力对话的长度，利于检测学生的综合能力。第三部分是"读"，从Task 7到Task 11，涉及图表类和应用类文本阅读等五个任务，内容包括介绍职业、杰出人物、传统节日、志愿服务和科技创新等。第四部分是"写"，一个任务，即Task 12，内容为写一篇介绍家乡的说明文。

四部分难易度比例为7：2：1，基础题占比70%，中等难度题占比20%，稍高难度题占比10%。

Speaking（Task 1–Task 3，共20分）

【题型分析】“说”的部分为学生设计通用的生活或职业场景，创设英语口语使用情境，涉及“科学与技术”“社会交往”“学习与生活”等主题，引导学生进行英语口语互动交流，通过反复朗读潜移默化地培养语感，帮助学生形成优美的语言和动听的语调，达到职场语言沟通和跨文化理解的核心素养培养目标。

本部分有朗读词汇、朗读情景对话和朗读短文三个任务。它们聚焦不同主题，创设相应情境，由易到难。Task 1考查学生朗读词汇的能力，要求学生能正确清晰地发音。Task 2考查学生朗读短对话的能力，要求学生根据职业场景扮演角色，朗读角色对应的对话内容，能在情境中简要描述人物、活动、事件和经历等，促进其职场语言沟通能力的提升。Task 3考查学生朗读短篇段落的能力，要求学生在有准备的情况下能就熟悉的话题进行简单陈述，提升其职场语言沟通能力和思维差异感知能力。

Task 1

You are working in the field of science and technology. You are telling people about the great inventions. Read the following inventions. (0.5×10=5 points) 你是一位科技工作者，正在讲解给人类生活带来巨变的伟大发明。请将以下发明大声读出来。

1. paper-making	2. printing
3. compass	4. gunpowder
5. high-speed train	6. online shopping
7. bike-sharing	8. WeChat
9. smartphone	10. Internet of Things

【解析】本任务聚焦《课程标准》基础模块“科学与技术”的主题，创设科技工作人员讲解科技发明的情境，要求学生能够正确朗读与科技相关的单词和短语，能就与科技相关的话题进行有效沟通与交流，促进学生职场语言沟通能力的提升，同时引导学生感受中国科技的发展和巨变，坚定科技强国信心。

Task 2

You are Li Ying. You are talking about your internship with your partner. Read the conversation and tell others about your internship. (5 points) 你叫李颖，正在与同伴谈论你的实习。请读出对话，告诉大家你的实习情况。

Partner: Li Ying, what do you do in your internship?

Li Ying: First I've finished the pre-service training and learnt a lot about working in a real hotel. Now I am an assistant receptionist.

Partner: Tell me more.

Li Ying: Well, I receive guests, help with check-in and checkout, and pick up telephones.

Partner: Do you get along well with your workmates?

Li Ying: Of course! We're friends now.

【解析】本任务聚焦《课程标准》基础模块“社会交往”的主题，创设李华在酒店实习的职业场景，要求学生扮演角色，朗读短对话，简要谈论酒店服务的工作内容，能运用有关办理入住、退房等的表述进行沟通和交流，提升职场语言沟通能力，引导学生感受服务行业的劳动精神和工匠精神，为提升个人综合素养打下基础。

Task 3

You are going to give a speech about how to manage time. Read the speech to tell people what you think. (10 points) 你将做一场关于时间管理的演讲。请大声读出你的演讲词。

It is important to manage your time. Here are some tips.

Follow a daily schedule. You'd better make a to-do list first. It should be in order of importance. Do important tasks first.

Make it manageable. Tick items off after you have finished them. Break the task into small parts if it's big. Then decide how long you need to spend on each part, depending on the deadline.

Focus on your tasks. If possible, turn your phone off. Phones can take up a lot of time. Meanwhile, you can try some time management apps to help you stay focused.

Everyone can become better at managing time. Like everything else, it just takes practice!

【解析】本任务聚焦《课程标准》基础模块“学习与生活”的主题，创设就时间管理进行演讲的情境，要求学生朗读时间管理的演讲词，能就时间管理的话题进行简单陈述，为学生应对头绪繁多的学习和生活提供指导，帮助学生提升学习效率、优化学习方法，达到培养学生职场语言沟通和思维差异感知的核心素养目标。

Listening （Task 4–Task 6，共20分）

【题型分析】“听”的部分为学生设计通用的生活或职业场景，让学生以参与者或职业人身份进入情境，涉及“自我与他人”“学习与生活”“社会服务”等主题。学生在创设的真实情境中，听音频并获取信息，根据生活或职场任务的要求处理信息，从而实现有效交流。本部分旨在考查学生获取信息的能力，以及对获取的信息进行分析、归纳、总结并得出结论或发表自己看法的能力。

本部分包含听句子、听短对话和听长对话三个任务。它们聚焦不同主题，创设相应情境，由易到难。Task 4是基础题，考查学生听简单语句做出适当反应的能力，在具体情境中提升学生职场语言沟通能力。Task 5属于中档题，考查学生从简短对话中提取时间、数字、主题等相关信息的能力，帮助学生通过筛选关键信息提升其思维差异感知能力和自主学习能力。Task 6属于稍高难度题，考查学生理解长对话的主旨、辨别说话者的态度等语言运用能力，在对比、辨别和理解中提升学生思维差异感知能力、跨文化理解能力和自主学习能力。

Task 4

You are a student from Huaxia Vocational School. Your new friend Peter is asking you some questions about you and your family. You are going to hear five questions. Listen carefully and respond. Each question will be read twice. (1×5=5 points) 你是华夏职业学校的学生。你的新朋友彼得正在询问你和你家人的情况。你将听到5个问题。请听提问并做出回应。每个问题读两遍。

Question 1: How old are you?

(　　) 1. A. I'm 17 years old.
B. I'm from Chongqing.
C. I'm good at basketball.

Question 2: How do you usually go to school?

(　　) 2. A. I usually get up at 6:30 am.
B. I usually walk to school.
C. I usually have an egg for breakfast.

Question 3: What do you do with your family?

(　　) 3. A. We often read books.
B. We are well-built.
C. We always feel happy.

Question 4: Do you have brothers or sisters?

(　　) 4. A. Yes, my brothers are at home.
B. No, my sisters are very helpful.
C. Yes, I have a younger brother.

Question 5: Which subject do you like best?

(　　) 5. A. My favourite subject is history.

B. I major in e-commerce.

C. I practise my skills in the workshop.

【解析】本任务聚焦《课程标准》基础模块“自我与他人”的主题，创设关于家庭生活的简短对话情境，要求学生能听懂关于家庭成员和家庭生活的问句并做出适当回应，选出正确答语，引导学生在日常家庭生活中理解中华家风，传承好家风。

Task 5

You are a salesman of a clothing store. A customer is buying clothes. Choose the right information according to the conversation. The conversation will be read twice. (1×5=5 points) 你是一家服装店的销售人员。一位顾客正在买衣服。请根据对话内容选择正确信息。对话读两遍。

Salesman: *Good afternoon. May I help you?*

Customer: *Yes, I'd like to buy a dress. Do you have this dress in other colours?*

Salesman: *Yes, they come in four colours: red, yellow, pink and white.*

Customer: *Do you have a white one in size M?*

Salesman: *One moment, I'll check... Yes, we do. Here you are.*

Customer: *It looks nice. What is it made of?*

Salesman: *It's made of silk. It's the latest style.*

Customer: *How much is it?*

Salesman: *It's 1000 yuan. But today there's a special 90% discount for anything over 500 yuan, so it's 900 yuan.*

Customer: *I'd like to take this dress. Can I pay by WeChat?*

Salesman: *Sure. Please show your QR code.*

(　　) 1. What does the customer want to buy?

A. A skirt.　　B. A dress.　　C. A scarf.

(　　) 2. How many colours are mentioned in the conversation?

A. Two.　　B. Three.　　C. Four.

(　　) 3. What size does the customer want to have?

A. Size S.　　B. Size M.　　C. Size L.

(　　) 4. How much will the customer pay for the dress?

A. 1000 *yuan*.　　B. 900 *yuan*.　　C. 500 *yuan*.

(　　) 5. How will the customer pay the bill?

A. By WeChat.　　B. By cash.　　C. By Alipay.

【解析】本任务聚焦《课程标准》基础模块“学习与生活”的主题，创设在服装店购物的情境，要求学生能听懂关于购物的简短对话，提取出购买物品、价格、支付方式等关键信息，能理解购物常用语，如询问颜色、价格、尺码、数量、付款方式、材质等的问答语，选择正确答案，帮助学生在购物中培养服务意识和沟通意识，提高跨文化理解能力和职场语言沟通能力。

Task 6

You are a nurse who is working in a school clinic. Listen to the conversation between the doctor and Li Ming, and finish the recording. The conversation will be read twice. (2×5=10 points) 你是学校医务室的护士。请听医生与李明的对话，完成李明的就诊记录单。对话读两遍。

Li Ming: *Good morning, sir. Here is my appointment number.*

Doctor: *Thank you. So what's wrong with you?*

Li Ming: *I have a sore throat and a terrible cough. My temperature is over 38℃.*

Doctor: *I see. How long have you been like this?*

Li Ming: *Since yesterday morning.*

Doctor: *Please open your mouth and say "Ah". Hmm, I'm afraid you have a cold.*

Li Ming: *Is it serious? I feel really bad.*

Doctor: *Don't worry. It's nothing serious. Take this medicine one tablet each time and three times a day, drink more water and do have a good rest.*

Li Ming: *What else should I do?*

Doctor: *Have light food. And when you feel better, do more exercise.*

Li Ming: *Thank you. I see.*

What's wrong with Li Ming?	
Symptoms	Have a sore throat and a terrible 1. _______ The temperature is over 2. _______ ℃
How long	Since yesterday morning
Diagnosis	Have a 3. _______
Suggestions	Take this medicine one tablet each time and 4. _______ times a day. Have 5. _______ food and do more exercise.

【解析】本任务聚焦《课程标准》基础模块“学习与生活”的主题，创设生病就医的情境，要求学生能听懂关于生病就诊的长对话，提取关键信息，填写简单的就诊记录单（如生病症状、医生诊断、服药事项等），准确写出相关数字或单词，帮助学生在理解就诊对话的过程中增强跨文化理解能力和职场语言沟通能力，树立强身健体意识，养成良好的生活习惯，为将来生活、工作打下坚实基础。

Reading （Task 7–Task 11，共50分）

【题型分析】“读”的部分为学生设计生活或职场常见的图表、文本等，让学生通过看图表、读语篇等阅读活动获取信息，并通过分析、梳理、归纳信息实现信息转换，完成生活或职场交际任务。本部分包含图表类和应用类文本阅读等五个任务，聚焦“求职应聘”“职业规划”“科学与技术”“历史与文化”“社会服务”“技术应用”等不同主题，创设相应情境，形式多样，内容丰富，难度适中。Task 7为看图片匹配文字题，要求学生能看懂图片并与相关职业进行匹配，增强职场语言沟通能力。Task 8为提取文本信息完成信息卡题，要求学生能从主题熟悉的文本中找到特定信息，完成人物简介，增强自主学习能力。Task 9为根据信息补全语篇题，要求学生能读懂常见的活动要素的表述并理解信息关联，完成短文填空，增强跨文化理解能力和自主学习能力。Task 10为招聘启事的应用类文本，要求学生提取信息并选择正确答案，增强职场语言沟通能力。Task 11为根据表格信息选择正确答案题，要求学生能在表格中找出特定信息，理解主旨，做出推论，增强自主学习能力。

Task 7

You are a teacher in a vocational school. You are introducing different jobs to students. Match the jobs to the pictures. (2×5=10 points) 你是职业学校的教师，正在给学生做就业指导。请将下列工作内容与对应的图片配对。

A. checking circuits	B. designing clothes	C. repairing cars
D. welding steel	E. introducing tea	

1. ________

2. ________

3. ________

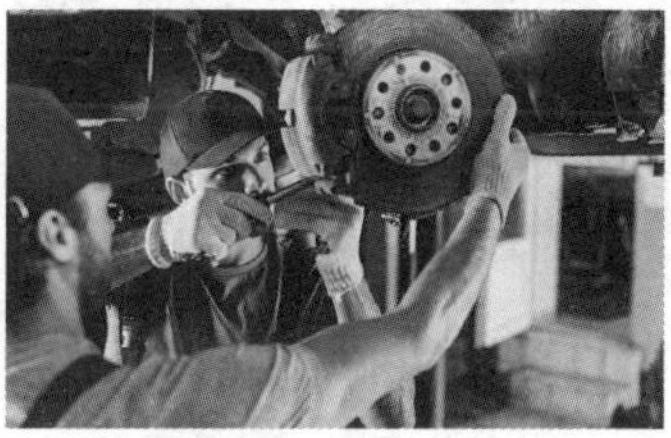

4. ________

5. ________

1. ________ 2. ________ 3. ________
4. ________ 5. ________

【解析】本任务聚焦《课程标准》职业模块“求职应聘”和“职业规划”的主题，创设职业指导情境，要求学生能看懂相关工作场景的图片，理解相关的词汇，做出合乎逻辑的推论，匹配与词汇所展示情境相同的图片，完成练习。学生在完成练习的过程中，感受各行各业的职业之美、劳动之美、创造之美，增强跨文化理解能力和职场语言沟通能力。

Task 8

You are a staff member of the Great Exhibition Centre. You are preparing for an exhibition about great scientists. Read the introduction of Tu Youyou and complete the information card. (2×5=10 points) 你是展览中心的工作人员，正在准备杰出科学家人物展。请根据屠呦呦的人物介绍填写人物信息卡。

Tu Youyou is one of the greatest scientists in China. In December, 1930, Tu Youyou was born in Ningbo, Zhejiang province. In 1951, she attended Beijing Medical College. Tu Youyou read hundreds of ancient medical texts and carried out thousands of experiments to find the anti-malarial substance called artemisinin (青蒿素) to save people's lives. She set a good example for her team. She was never satisfied with her work and always perfected the drug she discovered. In 2015, she was awarded the Nobel Prize. In September, 2019, she was awarded the Medal of the Republic.

Tu Youyou	
Date and place of birth	Tu Youyou was born in Ningbo in 1. ________.
Career	She is a doctor and medical scientist.
In 1951	She attended 2. ________.
Contribution (贡献)	She found the anti-malarial substance called 3. ________.
In 2015	She was awarded the 4. ________.
In September, 2019	She was awarded the 5. ________.

【解析】本任务聚焦《课程标准》基础模块“科学与技术”的主题，创设著名科学家人物展情境，要求学生读懂关于诺贝尔奖获得者屠呦呦的人物介绍，提取数字、事件、主题等特定信息，完成人物信息卡的填写，帮助学生在情境中感受科技给人类带来的改变，萌发对伟大人物的崇敬与爱戴，树立技能立身、技能报国的信心，增强思维差异感知能力和跨文化理解能力。

Task 9

You are the chairman of the student union in Xingguang Vocational School. You are preparing for an activity about the Dragon Boat Festival. Read the information below and complete the notice. (1×10=10 points) 你是星光职业学校学生会主席，正在准备端午节的一项活动。请阅读以下信息并完成通知。

Theme	Food and traditional festivals
Time	15:30–17:00, this Wednesday
Activity	◆ share your stories about food and festivals ◆ make *zongzi* with your friends together
Place	at Happy Café
People	anyone interested
How to apply	log on to the school's official website before 21 June

Notice

The Dragon Boat Festival is coming. In order to 1. ________ (promote) traditional Chinese culture, some 2. ________ (activity) about the Dragon Boat Festival will be 3. ________ (hold). The 4. ________ of the activities is "Food and traditional festivals". You are welcome to 5.________ (share) your stories about food and festivals. After that, you can make 6. ________ with your friends together. Anyone 7. ________ (interest) is welcome to join the activities from 15:30 8. ________ 17:00 this Wednesday at Happy Café. You should log on to the school's official 9. ________ before 21 June to 10. ________ (apply).

Looking forward to your attendance.

The Student Union

19 June

【解析】本任务聚焦《课程标准》基础模块"历史与文化"的主题，创设学校庆祝端午节活动的情境，要求学生能读懂关于端午节的活动安排，提取特定信息，根据提示或关键词转述文本大意，补全通知内容。学生在简要介绍端午节的情境中，提升思维差异感知能力和跨文化理解能力。

Task 10

You are the chairman of the student union in Sunshine School. You need to answer the questions from your schoolmates about "Volunteers wanted". (2×5=10 points) 你是阳光学校的学生会主席。你正在就学校的志愿者招募启事进行答疑。请根据要求解答校友们的提问。

Volunteers wanted

Do you want to do something to protect the earth?

Volunteers are needed for our earth protection activity this Sunday at Green Park.

Work includes:

- picking up rubbish in the park
- helping recycle plastics
- telling people how to sort waste
- planting trees

You need to be:

- interested in protecting the earth
- at least 16 years old
- able to work from 9:00 am to 5:00 pm this Sunday

You can:

- make new friends
- get a certificate

Contact us for more information at volunteer@123123.com.

(　　) 1. When will the activity be held?

A. This Sunday.　　B. This Wednesday.　　C. This weekend.

(　　) 2. Where will the activity be held?

A. On the playground.　　B. At the school gym.　　C. At Green Park.

(　　) 3. How can we get more information?

A. By telephone.　　B. By email.　　C. By letter.

(　　) 4. During the activity, what will the volunteers do?

A. They will pick up rubbish in the park.

B. They will tell people how to sort waste.

C. Both A and B.

(　　) 5. Which is required to be a volunteer?

A. They should be at least 18 years old.

B. They should be able to work from 9:00 am to 5:00 pm this Sunday.

C. They should be strong enough to help people.

【**解析**】本任务聚焦《课程标准》基础模块“社会服务”的主题，创设学校志愿者招募答疑活动情境，要求学生能读懂志愿者招募的相关要求，找到时间、地点、方式等特定信息，理解招募主旨，根据招募信息做出推论，完成答案选择。学生通过读招募启事和完成任务，理解奉献、友爱、互助的青年志愿者精神，提升思维差异感知能力和自主学习能力。

Task 11

You are a staff member of a science and technology museum. You are responsible for offering help or instructions to the visitors according to the museum's arrangement. (2×5=10 points) 你是某科技博物馆的工作人员，负责根据博物馆的工作安排为参观者提供帮助或指导。

Science and technology museum				
Floor	Theme	Example	Features	Time
The first floor	The glory of china	the china we use	beautiful and useful	9:00—16:00
The second floor	Challenges and future	wind generator	green and dean	
The third floor	Science, technology and life	solar lamps	handy and eco-friendly	
Notice: Available from Tuesdays to Sundays (closed on Mondays)				

(　　) 1. Where is the exhibition held?

A. At a science and technology museum.

B. At a science and life museum.

C. At a technology and life museum.

(　　) 2. When can people visit the exhibition?

A. At 10:00 on Mondays.

B. At 14:00 on Fridays.

C. At 17:00 on Sundays.

(　　) 3. What is the theme of the second floor?

A. The glory of china.

B. Challenges and future.

C. Science, technology and life.

(　　) 4. Where can we find the china we use?

A. On the first floor.

B. On the second floor.

C. On the third floor.

(　　) 5. What do people think of the solar lamps?

A. They are beautiful and useful.

B. They are green and clean.

C. They are handy and eco-friendly.

【解析】本任务聚焦《课程标准》基础模块“科学与技术”和职业模块“技术应用”的主题，创设科技博物馆的讲解工作情境，要求学生能读懂科技馆的日常安排，提取数字、主旨等关键信息，梳理、归纳信息，完成选择，帮助学生在答疑的过程中，感悟科技带给我们的便捷与舒适，体会创新的力量，理解终身学习的意义，提升思维差异感知能力和自主学习能力。

Writing （Task 12，共10分）

【题型分析】“写”的部分为学生设计常见的生活或职业场景，要求学生根据提供的信息或场景要求，完成写作任务。本部分包含一个任务，聚焦学生熟悉的日常生活或职业场景，涉及《课程标准》中的八大主题，以应用文类和记叙文类为主。要求学生能用简短语言介绍自己、家人或家乡，能简要介绍活动、事件、节日或经历等，能在对方帮助下记录简短信息，能写出简单的通知、请假条、求职信、个人职业规划等应用类短文，从而提升思维差异感知能力、跨文化理解能力和自主学习能力。

Task 12

You are Li Hua, a tour guide of Good Times Travel Agency. You want to introduce your hometown—Chongqing to your friend Sarah. Complete the introduction about Chongqing according to the clues. (15 points) 你是美好时光旅行社的导游李华。你想为朋友萨拉介绍自己的家乡——重庆。请根据以下提示向你的朋友推介重庆。

An introduction about Chongqing	
Location	southwest of China
Nickname	the Mountain City
What to do	◆ visit an ancient town–Ciqikou ◆ enjoy the night view at Hongya Cave ◆ see the light rail go through the building at Liziba
Delicacies	◆ hot pot ◆ noodles

Hey Sarah,

I'm really glad to tell you something about Chongqing. ______________

____

____

____

____.

A nice city, isn't it?

Yours sincerely,

Li Hua

【解析】本任务聚焦《课程标准》基础模块“学习与生活”的主题，创设为外国好友介绍家乡的情境，要求学生能读懂表格中的地理位置、景点、美食等信息，用简单的语言介绍自己的家乡。学生在介绍家乡的过程中，感受家乡人文之美、物产之美，增强对家乡的了解与热爱，提升跨文化理解能力和自主学习能力。

评价检测解析（基础模块二）写作范文

Hey Sarah,

I'm really glad to tell you something about Chongqing. It lies in the southwest of China. There are many mountains in Chongqing, so it is also called the Mountain City. Chongqing is a magical city. Here you can visit an ancient town named Ciqikou. You can also enjoy the night view at Hongya Cave. Many people are interested in seeing the light rail go through the building at Liziba. I believe it will impress you. What's more, hot pot and noodles are delicacies of Chongqing. They are very popular. Don't miss them.

A nice city, isn't it?

Yours sincerely,

Li Hua

五 探索符合新课标的检测任务内容专项范例

新课标理念下的口语专项检测范例

（一）

Task 1

Yesterday was your first day at work. It was so meaningful for you. You wrote down what you did yesterday to share them with your friends. Read the following expressions loudly. (0.5×10=5 points) 昨天是你入职的第一天，这对你来说意义重大。你将昨天所做的事都记录下来和你的朋友分享。请将以下表述大声读出来。

1. get up
2. go to work by subway
3. meet the HR
4. meet the co-workers
5. introduce myself
6. take a tour
7. have lunch
8. have some training
9. prepare for a tea break
10. join a meeting

Task 2

You are Li Hua and you are working in a shoe shop. Now you are helping a customer to find a pair of shoes she loves. Read the conversation loudly. (5 points) 你叫李华，在一家鞋店工作。你正在帮助顾客找一双她心仪的鞋子。请大声读出对话。

Li Hua: Good morning, Madam. Welcome to our store. What can I do for you?

Customer: Yes, please. I'd like to buy a pair of sports shoes.

Li Hua: How about these black and white ones? They are so comfortable to wear. And they are on sale today.

Customer: Oh, they look nice. How much are they?

Li Hua: One hundred *yuan*.

Task 3

You are Li Hua, a teacher in a vocational school. In your class, half of the students seldom share their life stories with their parents. You want them to be friends with their parents. So you share one of your family stories with them. Read the story loudly to your students. (10 points) 你是李华，一名职业学校的老师。在你们班有一半的学生很少和家长分享他们的生活。你想让学生们和家长做朋友。因此你跟他们分享了你的一个家庭故事。请大声读出你的故事。

> This is a photo of my family. The man who looks well-built is my father. Beside him, the woman with grey hair is my mum. I look like my father and we have the same wide smile. This is my brother. We're close. He is a good listener. He is kind and hard-working. My family like sports, so we often do sport outdoors together. My brother was teaching me to ride a bike while my parents were taking pictures. We always have fun together.

（二）

Task 1

You are a teacher in a primary school. You are telling your students about some inventions. Read the following inventions loudly. (0.5×10=5 points) 你是一名小学老师，正在给学生们讲解一些创新发明。请将以下发明大声读出来。

1. paper-making
2. printing
3. compass
4. gunpowder
5. online shopping
6. mobile payment
7. high-speed railway
8. bike sharing
9. hybrid rice
10. e-commerce

Task 2

You are Li Hua, studying at a vocational school. Now you are talking about the school's science festival with your friend Penny. Read the conversation loudly. (5 points) 你叫李华，在一所职业学校学习。你正在与朋友彭妮谈论学校的科学节。请大声读出对话。

Penny: Hey, Li Hua. How was the science festival?

Li Hua: It was great! What the students showed was amazing. I really enjoyed it.

Penny: What did you do at the festival?

Li Hua: Our group took part in an activity. We made a robot which could dance to music.

Penny: That's wonderful. It must have improved your team spirit.

Li Hua: Yes, and also my practical skills.

Task 3

You are a doctor in People's Hospital. Now you are giving a speech in a vocational school. You are talking to the students to help them form good habits. Read the speech loudly. (10 points) 你是人民医院的一名医生。你正在一所职业学校给学生们做演讲，帮助学生养成良好习惯。请大声读出你的演讲内容。

> Good morning, everyone. I'm Doctor Li from People's Hospital. I've heard that some of you like playing computer games for a long time. You stay up late to play more games. But do you feel tired in the daytime? Do you have a backache sometimes? Yes, of course. You need to try to become better. First, play computer games for less time. Then, go to bed on time and have a good sleep. It'll help you learn well and stay healthy.

新课标理念下的听力专项检测范例

（一）

Task 1

You are a tour guide from Sunshine Travel Agency. You are giving an introduction about Chongqing to a group of foreigners. You are going to hear five questions from them. Listen carefully and respond. Each question will be read twice. (1×5=5 points) 你是来自阳光旅行社的一名导游，正在给一群外国人介绍重庆。你会听到游客的5个问题。请听提问并做出回应。每个问题读两遍。

(　　) 1. A. It is a city with a special history.
B. In southwest China.
C. It's really worth visiting.

(　　) 2. A. Mountains and rivers.
B. Friendly, warm-hearted and hard-working.
C. Modern life.

(　　) 3. A. That sounds interesting.
B. To learn about different cultures.
C. There are many beautiful places. It is most famous for Hechuan Fishing Town.

(　　) 4. A. Sounds great.
B. Any suggestions?
C. It's a city with higher temperatures in summer.

(　　) 5. A. Yes. Chongqing is called the Mountain City and the Foggy City.
B. That's impossible.
C. I'm afraid I have no time.

Task 2

You are Jerry, a student of a vocational school. Now you don't feel well and you are seeing a doctor. Choose the right information according to the conversation. The conversation will be read twice. (1×5=5 points) 你是杰瑞，一所职业学校的学生。你生病了，正在看医生。请根据对话内容选择正确信息。对话读两遍。

(　　) 1. What is the conversation about?
A. Seeing a doctor.　　B. Interviewing.　　C. Chatting.

(　　) 2. What's wrong with Jerry?
A. Taking a seat.　　B. Having a terrible headache.
C. Having a fever.

(　　) 3. What's the doctor's suggestion?

A. Going on working.

B. Not mentioned.

C. Taking some medicine.

(　　) 4. How long has Jerry been ill?

A. About two days. B. A week. C. He doesn't know.

(　　) 5. In the doctor's opinion, how will Jerry feel in a few days?

A. Not sure. B. Worse. C. Better.

Task 3

Han Yu, a vocational school student in China, is talking about her volunteer work with her friend Wu Lin. Listen to their conversation and make notes. The conversation will be read twice. (2×5=10 points) 韩玉是中国一所职业学校的学生，正在和朋友吴林谈论她的志愿工作。请听他们的对话并完成表格记录。对话读两遍。

Volunteer work information	
Where Han Yu is doing volunteer work	at a __1__ home
Volunteers' duties	__2__ with children, chatting with the elderly and __3__ up rubbish
Requirements	being __4__ to help having good __5__ skills

（二）

Task 1

You are shopping now in the sports section in a department store. A shop assistant is serving you. You are going to hear five questions from the assistant. Listen carefully and respond. Each question will be read twice. (1×5=5 points) 你正在一家购物商场的运动专区购物。一位商场营业员正在为你

服务。你会听到营业员的5个问题。请听提问并做出回应。每个问题读两遍。

(　　) 1. A. Welcome to our store.
B. I'm looking for a pair of sports shoes.
C. It's made of silk.

(　　) 2. A. I'm afraid I have no cash with me.
B. It's the best seller.
C. I'm interested in running shoes.

(　　) 3. A. It's cheaper.
B. Size 36.
C. Keeping fit.

(　　) 4. A. White.
B. Wait a moment, please.
C. It is popular.

(　　) 5. A. Mobile payment.
B. It's convenient.
C. It is the latest style.

Task 2

You are Wang Lei, a student of a vocational school. You are talking about role models of the time with your classmate Li Ying. Choose the right information according to the conversation. The conversation will be read twice. (1×5=5 points) 你是王雷，一所职业学校的学生。你正在和同学李颖谈论时代的楷模。请根据对话内容选择正确信息。对话读两遍。

(　　) 1. Who are Wang Lei and Li Ying talking about?
A. Respectable scientists and craftsmen.
B. Excellent players.
C. Great actors.

(　　) 2. Why was Yuan Longping respected according to the conversation?
A. He had a great deal of energy.
B. He provided a solution to worldwide hunger.
C. Because he won so many prizes.

(　　) 3. Are many of their classmates fans of Yuan Longping, Tu Youyou and Gao Fenglin?
A. No, they aren't.　　B. Not mentioned.　　C. Yes, they are.

(　　) 4. What is mentioned in the conversation?
A. Scientists and craftsmen have contributed a lot to our country.
B. Scientists and craftsmen are strong-willed.
C. Scientists are fans of skilled craftsmen.

(　　) 5. What will one of the speakers plan to be in the future?
A. Not sure.
B. A successful person.
C. A professional person.

Task 3

Lily is an assistant of Professor Li. A visitor is asking her on the phone to make an appointment with Professor Li. Listen to their conversation and make notes. The conversation will be read twice. (2×5=10 points) 莉莉是李教授的助理。一位来访者在电话里和她确定与李教授的见面时间。请听来访者与莉莉的对话，完成表格记录。对话读两遍。

Key information	
Telephone time between Lily and the visitor	in the 1. ________
Visitor's name	2. ________ Brown
Available appointment time	at 3. ________ tomorrow

What Professor Li will do tomorrow morning	give a 4. ________
Meeting place	Professor Li's 5. ________

新课标理念下的阅读专项检测范例

（一）

Task 1

The Spring Festival is approaching. You and your family are planning activities for the festival. Match the activities with the pictures. (2×5=10 points) 春节即将来临，你和家人在计划春节的活动，请将下列活动与对应的图片配对。

A. go shopping	B. have a family party	C. have a picnic
D. visit friends and relatives	E. climb mountains	

1. ________

2. ________

3. ________

4. ________

5. ________

1. ________ 2. ________ 3. ________
4. ________ 5. ________

Task 2

You are preparing a video to introduce China's four new inventions and the changes they have brought to people's lives. Complete the information card according to the introduction. (2×5=10 points) 你在准备一段视频，介绍中国新四大发明及其带给人们生活的变化。请根据下面的介绍填写信息卡。

High-speed railway, mobile payment, bike sharing and online shopping are the four great new inventions in China.

Chinese high-speed railway is famous for its speed and comfort. We have the world's longest high-speed railway network and have exported our railway technology to other countries.

Mobile payment is common in China, and people can meet various payment needs without cash. Mobile payment has promoted the growth of the digital economy.

Bike sharing has solved the problem of the last-mile transportation. Through smartphone applications, users can easily rent and return bikes, a model that has been used in cities around the world.

Online shopping has completely changed people's shopping habits. Online shopping platforms provide a convenient shopping experience, a wide range of product options, and efficient logistics (物流) services.

The four great new inventions in China

Inventions	Advantages
High-speed railway	known for 1. ________, comfort, and extensive network
Mobile payment	can meet various payment needs 2. ________ cash
Bike sharing	a model 3. ________ has been 4. ________ in cities around the world
Online shopping	has 5. ________ changed people's shopping habits

Task 3

You are the Health Committee member in your class and now you are preparing a poster on preventing flu (流感). Complete the poster according to the information given. (1×10=10 points) 你是班上的卫生委员，正在做一期预防流感的健康知识海报。请根据所给信息完成海报。

Prevention tip	Description
Wash hands	Use soap and wash for at least 20 seconds, especially after being in public places or before eating.
Cover your mouth and nose when coughing/sneezing	Use paper and dispose of it properly.
Keep a safe social distance	Avoid close contact with sick people and keep away from others if you're ill.
Eat a balanced diet	Include fruit and vegetables.
Have a good sleep and do exercise	Get enough sleep and do exercise regularly to strengthen your body.
Get a flu shot (注射)	If advised by your healthcare provider

Tips on flu prevention

As the weather is getting colder and colder, it's important to protect ourselves from the flu. Here are some simple tips to stay healthy.

☆ Wash your hands often with soap and warm water for at least 1. _________ seconds, especially after being 2. _________ public places or before eating.

☆ Cover your mouth and nose with paper 3. _________ you cough or sneeze, and dispose of it properly.

☆ Avoid close contact 4. _________ people who are sick. If you are ill, 5. _________ away from others to prevent the virus (病毒).

☆ Eat a 6. _________ diet rich in fruit 7. _________ vegetables.

☆ Get 8. _________ sleep and exercise regularly to keep a strong body that can fight off germs.

☆ Consider 9. _________ a flu shot (疫苗) if 10. _________ by your doctor.

By following these easy tips, we can all help reduce the spread of the flu this season.

Task 4

Li Ming is sixteen years old. He has a bad cold and coughs (咳嗽) day and night. The doctor gives him some cough medicine. Help him to take the medicine properly according to the instruction by answering the questions. (2×5=10 points) 李明16岁了，因为得了重感冒咳嗽得厉害。医生给他开了一些咳嗽药。请根据药品说明书，协助他回答下列问题，以便清楚如何服药。

Cough medicine

Shake it well before use. Take it three times each day before meals.

Age	**Dose (药量) each time**
over 15	2 teaspoonfuls (勺)
8～14	1 teaspoonful
4～7	1/2 teaspoonful

Not right for children below the age of three. Put it in a cold place. Use it before 1 December 2026.

(　　) 1. What should be done before taking the medicine?

A. Take the temperature.

B. Shake it well.

C. Clear the running nose.

(　　) 2. How many times should the medicine be taken a day?

A. Two times.　　B. Three times.　　C. Four times.

(　　) 3. How many teaspoonfuls should be taken every day for a person aged 16?

A. 2 teaspoonfuls.　　B. 4 teaspoonfuls.　　C. 6 teaspoonfuls.

(　　) 4. Where should the medicine be kept?

A. In a fridge.　　B. Under the sun.　　C. In any place.

(　　) 5. If now it is 2 June 2027, what should be done to the medicine?

A. Be thrown away.　　B. Be taken as usual.　　C. Be kept in a fridge.

Task 5

You are doing volunteer work in a museum. You are telling visitors the changes upon our lives because of technology development. Answer the visitors' questions according to the following information. (2×5=10 points) 你是博物馆的志愿讲解员，正在给参观者讲解技术改变生活的实例。请根据以下信息回答参观者的问题。

Technology is developing so fast that many things commonly used in the past have faded out of sight today. Let's look at three of the things and see what happened to them.

Aspect	In the past	Nowadays
Television	We used to watch black and white televisions which could only show black and white pictures.	We watch colour televisions which show clear and colourful scenes.
Communication	People wrote letters to communicate with others and waited for weeks for a reply.	The Internet makes communication convenient and fast, even when the people are thousands of miles away.
Taking pictures	People used to carry big bags of film rolls to take pictures.	Digital cameras or mobile phones can be put into pockets, and people can almost take as many pictures as they want.

(　　) 1. What does the underlined phrase "out of sight" mean?

A. 消失不见　　B. 在外面　　C. 在心里

(　　) 2. What pictures did the black and white televisions show?

A. Clear and colourful pictures.

B. Black and white pictures.

C. Beautiful and interesting pictures.

(　　) 3. How did people communicate with others in the past?

A. By telephone.　　B. By email.　　C. By letter.

(　　) 4. What benefit does the Internet bring us?

A. It makes our communication convenient and fast.

B. People may wait for weeks for a reply.

C. It makes people live far away.

(　　) 5. What good sides do digital cameras and smartphones have?

A. They can be put into pockets.

B. They can almost help people take as many pictures as they want.

C. Both A and B.

(二)

Task 1

You are a tour guide and you are introducing some Chinese inventions to foreign tourists. Match the inventions to the pictures. (2×5=10 points) 你是一名导游，正给外国游客介绍一些中国的科技发明。请将下列发明与对应的图片配对。

A. the compass	B. high-speed railway	C. mobile payment
D. paper-making	E. shared bikes	

1. ______________

2. ______________

3. ______________

4. ______________

5. ______________

1. ____________ 2. ____________ 3. ____________
4. ____________ 5. ____________

Task 2

You are going to introduce the Weifang International Kite Festival. Read the passage and complete the information card. (2×5=10 points) 你准备介绍潍坊国际风筝节。请阅读下面的段落并完成有关风筝节的信息卡。

Weifang is in the eastern part of Shandong province. It's the hometown of kites in China. The kite, also called Zhiyuan or Zhiyao in ancient (古代的) China, has gone through over two thousand years of history. The ancient Chinese were making and flying kites even before they could write. A long time ago, the Chinese made kites to use in wars. They would fly these war kites in the dark. The kites were fixed so that they made strange sounds. Men who were at war with them would hear these sounds and run away. The ancient Chinese also flew kites to bring good luck and to make their crops grow rich and tall. The Weifang International Kite Festival is one of the most important kite sports events. It's an annual event, which falls in April every year. It has drawn thousands of visitors since it was first held in 1984. During the festival, you can see kites of all shapes, colours and sizes, and enjoy traditional folk songs, dance performances and fireworks shows.

Weifang International Kite Festival	
Place	Weifang, Shandong province
Time	1. _______ , every year
History	Kites are called Zhiyuan or Zhiyao in ancient China. They were used in 2. _______ or to bring 3. _______ and to make crops grow better. The Weifang International Kite Festival began in the year of 4. _______ .
Activity	See kites and enjoy traditional folk songs, dances and 5. _______

Task 3

You are a staff member in a hotel. Some foreigners in your hotel like Chinese food. You are introducing some restaurants to them. Read the chart below and give them some suggestions. (1×10=10 points) 你是某酒店的一名员工。你们酒店的一些外国人很喜欢中餐。你正在向他们介绍一些餐馆。请你根据以下图表内容给他们一些建议。

The House of Dumplings	best service, cheap and delicious
Sichuan Restaurant	best food, but a little expensive
Chinese Noodle Restaurant	cheapest, but with a long waiting time

There 1. ________ three restaurants near our hotel. Let me introduce them to you.

2. The ________ of the three restaurants is the House of Dumplings, 3. ________ is sure to have the 4. ________ (good) service. You will feel happy when you eat there. What's more, the food there is 5. ________ and cheap. Second, Sichuan Restaurant is 6. ________ (other) choice for you. Food there is the 7. ________ (good). I'm sure you will like it. But it's a little 8. ________ expensive than the other two. The last one is Chinese Noodle Restaurant. 9. ________ it's the cheapest, you may not enjoy it because 10. ________ a long waiting time.

I believe you can find your favourite restaurant. Hope you will enjoy it.

Task 4

You are Lily working in a volunteer organisation which now needs more volunteers. Answer the following questions according to "Volunteers wanted". (2×5=10 points) 你是志愿者莉莉。你所在的志愿组织目前需要更多的志愿者。请根据下面的招募启事，回答同学们的提问。

Volunteers wanted

Do you know the National Volunteer Week? Do you want to be a volunteer? More volunteers are wanted in our volunteer organisation.

National Volunteer Week

The National Volunteer Week started in 1974 and is held every April. It is a time to thank volunteers for their achievements. It is also a perfect opportunity (机会) to encourage others to take their first step toward becoming a volunteer.

Work includes:

Sing for the elderly at a nursing home

Tutor or just play with children at an orphanage

Pick up rubbish in a park

Hold a charity sale

Give directions to strangers

Time:

On Saturdays or Sundays

You need to:

Be patient.

Have free time at weekends.

Offer your help when and where you are needed. Remember the most important thing is to enjoy the volunteer experience.

(　　) 1. When did the National Volunteer Week start?

A. In 1974.　　B. In 1984.　　C. In 1994.

(　　) 2. What can people do during the National Volunteer Week?

A. Thank volunteers for their achievements.

B. Encourage others to take their first step toward becoming a volunteer.

C. Both A and B.

(　　) 3. What can we do as volunteers?

A. Sing for family members.

B. Play with children at an orphanage.

C. Give directions to classmates.

(　　) 4. When should we do the volunteer work?

A. On Saturdays or Sundays.

B. On Friday evenings.

C. Any time.

(　　) 5. What is the most important to do volunteer work?

A. To hold a charity sale.

B. To pick up rubbish in a park.

C. To enjoy the volunteer experience.

Task 5

You are listening to your friend who is sharing his role model. Answer the following questions according to the chart below. (2×5=10 points) 你正在听朋友分享他榜样的故事。请根据表格中提炼的人物信息，回答问题。

Facts about Qian Qihu	
Birthday	26 October 1937
Birthplace	Kunshan, China's Jiangsu province
Who he is	China's top defense engineering (国防工程) expert
What he has done	· He has spent more than 60 years studying and helping China build the "Underground Steel (钢铁) Great Wall". It works and provides protection when ground buildings are in trouble because of disasters or wars. · He has given away 8 million *yuan* to help poor children to receive education.
Awards (奖项)	· He was the winner of the State Preeminent Science and Technology Award in 2018. · He was awarded the August 1 Medal in 2022.

(　　) 1. When was Qian Qihu born?

A. He was born on 26 October 1937.

B. He was born on 26 November 1937.

C. He was born on 26 December 1937.

( ) 2. What did Qian Qihu do to help the poor children?

A. He taught them science and helped build schools for them.

B. He gave away 8 million *yuan* to help them receive education.

C. He spent 60 years helping them receive education.

( ) 3. What is Qian Qihu famous as?

A. He is famous as an excellent astronaut.

B. He is famous as a defense engineering expert.

C. He is famous as a good scientist.

( ) 4. When will the "Underground Steel Great Wall" work?

A. When there is a war.

B. When there is a disaster.

C. Both A and B.

( ) 5. What was Qian Qihu awarded in 2022?

A. He won the State Preeminent Science and Technology Award.

B. He was awarded the Medal of the Republic.

C. He was awarded the August 1 Medal.

新课标理念下的写作专项检测范例

（一）

Task

You are Lily who is a tour guide. You want to introduce amazing China to your foreign friend Tony. Read the following information and write a letter. (10 points) 你是导游莉莉，正在给你的外国朋友托尼推介大美中国。请根据以下信息写一封信，介绍这三个地方。

Amazing China		
Place	Specialties	Scenic spots
Beijing	roast duck	Great Wall Summer Palace
Sichuan	Zhuyeqing tea Zhangfei beef	Jiuzhaigou: beautiful water Wolong: cute pandas
Hangzhou	Longjing tea silk goods	West Lake Lingyin Temple

Dear Tony,

Do you know that there are so many beautiful and amazing places in China? Here I'll introduce three of them.

____

____

____

____

____

Welcome to China. I'm sure you'll fall in love with my country. Look forward to hearing from you.

Yours sincerely,

Lily

(二)

Task

You are Lily from the student union. You are writing a notice to look for volunteers to help the elderly. The following information should be included. (10 points) 你是学生会的莉莉，正在为寻找帮助老年人的志愿者写一份通知。通知需要包括以下信息。

Volunteers wanted	
When	winter holiday
Where	at a nursing home
Duties	sing for the elderly clean the rooms for the elderly chat with the elderly
Requirements	be patient be good at singing and dancing
More information	Contact us at volunteer@club.com.

Notice

Are you free in your winter holiday? ______________________________

____

____

____

____

____

六 探索落实学科核心素养及体现课程育人价值的综合检测任务示例

基于学科核心素养的综合检测任务

（一）

Speaking （Task 1–Task 3，共20分）

Task 1

You are a student and will graduate from a vocational school. On this Friday, you'll have an interview and introduce your character and appearance. Read the following terms loudly. (0.5×10=5 points) 你是一名即将毕业的职业学校学生。这周五你将参加一场面试，其间会介绍自己的性格和外貌。请将以下词汇大声读出来。

1. black hair
2. good-looking
3. easy-going
4. well-built
5. wide smile
6. cheerful
7. hard-working
8. narrow shoulders
9. lovely and smart
10. kind and helpful

Task 2

You are Zhang Ming. You are talking about your family members with your classmate Lily. Read the conversation loudly. (5 points) 你叫张明，正在与同学莉莉谈论你的家人。请大声读出以下对话。

Lily: Hello, Zhang Ming! Can you introduce your family to me?

Zhang Ming: Sure, Lily. This is a family photo of mine. The two people with grey hair are my grandparents.

Lily: Are these your parents?

Zhang Ming: Yes. They are my parents. They are very kind and always have wide smiles.

Lily: Is he your brother?

Zhang Ming: Yes. He is a lively boy.

Task 3

You are Wang Mei, a nurse in People's Hospital. Today you shared a blog on social media to help people stay away from flu. Read the blog loudly. (10 points) 你是王梅，人民医院的一名护士。今天你在社交软件上分享了一篇博文，提醒大家预防流感。请大声读出这篇博文。

> These days, it's becoming colder and colder. It's easy to get the flu. As we all know, flu can make many people sick. If you don't want to get the flu, what can you do? Firstly, keep the room clean and tidy, and open the windows to let the air in. Secondly, wash your hands with soap and running water. Thirdly, wear a mask when going out. Fourthly, do some exercise and get enough sleep.

Listening （Task 4–Task 6，共20分）

Task 4

You are a new student from Chongqing. Your teacher is asking you some questions about your hometown. You are going to hear five questions. Listen carefully and respond. Each question will be read twice. (1×5=5 points) 你是来自重庆的一名新生。你的老师正在询问你家乡的情况。你将听到5个问题。请听提问并做出回应。每个问题读两遍。

(　　) 1. A. I'm Li Ping.
B. I am from Chongqing.
C. I am 17 years old.

(　　) 2. A. You can enjoy mountains and rivers.
B. There are over 30 million people in Chongqing.
C. It is a city with a long history.

(　　) 3. A. There are many bridges in Chongqing.
B. The night scenery is beautiful.
C. Hard-working and friendly.

(　　) 4. A. Yes, I do.
B. No, you are right.
C. Welcome to Chongqing.

(　　) 5. A. Hot pot.
B. That's terrible.
C. I'm afraid I have no time.

Task 5

You are Jerry, a student of a vocational school. You are talking about your volunteer work with your classmate Li Ying. Choose the right information according to the conversation. The conversation will be read twice. (1×5=5 points) 你是杰瑞，一所职业学校的学生。你正在和同学李颖谈论你的志愿工作。请根据对话内容选择正确信息。对话读两遍。

(　　) 1. What is Jerry doing?
A. Doing some volunteer work.
B. Shopping.
C. Being on a holiday.

(　　) 2. Where does Jerry do the volunteer work?
A. At an animals' home.　　B. At a nursing home.　　C. At a children's home.

(　　) 3. Do the elderly want the volunteers to take care of them?
A. No, they don't.　　B. Not mentioned.　　C. Yes, they do.

(　　) 4. What do the volunteers do for the elderly in the conversation?
A. Play games with them.
B. Teach them to sing.
C. Help them to learn English.

(　　) 5. Will Li Ying join the volunteer work?
A. Not sure.　　B. No, she won't.　　C. Yes, she will.

Task 6

Lily is an assistant of the boss. She is asked to pick up an important guest at the airport. Listen to the conversation between Lily and her boss, and make notes. The conversation will be read twice. (2×5=10 points) 莉莉是老板助理。老板让她去机场接一位重要的客人。请听莉莉与老板的对话，完成会议记录。对话读两遍。

VIP information card	
Basic information	Mr Martin, a 1. _______ from New York University
Arrival time	at 2. _______ tomorrow
Flight number	3. _______
Hotel	4. _______ Hotel
Activity	holding a 5. _______ party for Mr Martin

Reading （Task 7–Task 11，共50分）

Task 7

You are a salesman in a supermarket. The Golden Week is coming. There will be a shopping festival in the supermarket. You need to put the promotion signs in the right places. Read the following terms and match them to the pictures. (2×5=10 points) 你是超市的售货员。黄金周就快到了，超市将举办一个购物节。你需要将活动标识放到对应的地方。请阅读以下优惠活动并将其与对应的图片配对。

A. buy 1 get 1 free	B. prize draw	C. free delivery
D. special offers	E. 50% discount	

1. ______________

2. ______________

3. ______________

4. ________　　　　5. ________

1. ________　2. ________　3. ________
4. ________　5. ________

Task 8

You are the host of a TV programme. You are preparing for a special programme about volunteers. Read the information and complete the card. (2×5=10 points) 你是某电视台主播，正在准备一期有关志愿者的专题节目。请根据下列信息填写信息卡。

Here is the information about four volunteer organisations:

The Chinese Young Volunteers Association (中国青年志愿者协会) was founded in 1994 by young people who were willing to devote themselves to social services. It is a national voluntary non-profit organisation.

The Red Cross Society of China (中国红十字会) was founded in 1904. The society has been involved in helping the refugees, assisting wounded soldiers, and providing assistance for disaster victims. The society also supports relief activities in other countries and regions.

The UN Volunteers (联合国志愿者) programme contributes to peace and development through volunteerism worldwide. The programme works with partners to promote the value and global recognition of volunteerism.

The World Wide Fund for Nature (世界自然基金会) is one of the world's leading conservation organisations. The fund works to protect forests and rivers, ensure a future for our precious wildlife, empower people and make our planet a better place for everyone.

Volunteer organisations	
Chinese Young Volunteers Association	It was founded in 1. _______ by young people who were willing to devote themselves to 2. _______.
Red Cross Society of China	It was founded in 3. _______.
UN Volunteers	The programme contributes to 4. _______ and development through volunteerism worldwide.
World Wide Fund for Nature	It works to protect forests and rivers... empower people and make our planet 5. _______ for everyone.

Task 9

You are the director of the Information Technology Department of the student union. You are preparing for the Science and Technology Festival. Complete the poster according to the information given. (1×10=10 points) 你是学生会信息技术部部长，正在筹备校园科技节活动。请根据所给信息完成海报。

Theme	Science and Technology Festival
Time	2:30 pm to 5:30 pm this Friday
Activity	students share ideas for new inventions
Place	Report Hall
People	anyone with new inventions
How to apply	upload works and instructions on the school website

Poster

The Science 1. _________ Technology Festival of our school this year is 2. _________ (come) . Are you interested 3. _________ joining us? It will bring you a new feeling.

Students 4. ________ (invite) to share ideas for new inventions. It will be very interesting. Last year, the best invention 5. ________ an anti-shaking spoon, designed especially for the 6. ________. It'll help seniors enjoy meals 7. ________ easily. 8. ________ one is an amazing invention—a straw 9. ________ filters water. It's really 10. ________ (use) for people who have no access to clean water. It's important that inventions benefit people's lives in some way.

Do you want to know if there will be better inventions this year? Come on, don't miss them!

Task 10

You are the chairman of the student union in Xingguang Vocational School. You are preparing for an activity named "How to manage your time". Read the chart below and answer the questions. (2×5=10 points) 你是星光职业学校的学生会主席，正在准备一项“如何管理你的时间”活动。请根据下面的表格回答问题。

Time	Activity
9:00–9:20	presentation by Peter Brown, headmaster
9:20–9:40	presentation by Jenny White, time management expert
9:40–10:00	break
10:00–10:30	group discussion
10:35–11:00	oral report

(　　) 1. Who will make a presentation at the beginning?

A. Jenny White.　　B. An expert.　　C. Peter Brown.

(　　) 2. What will the participants do at 9:50?

A. Discuss in groups.　　B. Take a break.　　C. Give an oral report.

(　　) 3. When will there be a group discussion?

A. From 10:00 to 10:30.

B. From 10:30 to 11:00.

C. From 9:40 to 10:00.

(　　) 4. There are _______ presentations in this activity.

A. Two.　　B. Three.　　C. Four.

(　　) 5. When will each group give an oral report?

A. At 10:00.　　B. At 10:15.　　C. At 10:35.

Task 11

These days the flu spreads quickly. As a student majoring in nursing, you are explaining the differences between the flu and the common cold. Answer the questions accordingly. (2×5=10 points) 近期流感频发。作为护理专业的学生，你正结合自身专业讲解流感和普通感冒的区别。请回答同学提问。

There are very important differences between the flu and a common cold.

Having a cold usually means having a running nose and a sore throat, along with an uncomfortable feeling in your chest. You'll probably keep sneezing and coughing. Unlike a common cold, the flu often gives you a big headache, a 3-day fever, and pains all over your body. And things can get even worse if this leads to pneumonia (肺炎). Children, the elderly or people with any other illness can easily catch it. It can even lead to death. But thankfully there is a vaccine against the flu. A shot (注射) will reduce your chances of getting the illness by 60%–80%.

More good news, the flu and a common cold have much in common. In both cases, you should drink plenty of water, juice and other healthy fluids. And get plenty of rest, so your body will be able to fight against viruses.

(　　) 1. Having a cold usually means having _______.

A. a running nose　　B. a sore throat　　C. both A and B

(　　) 2. Having flu often gives you _______.

A. a big headache　　B. a 3-day fever　　C. both A and B

(　　) 3. Which is the best way to keep away from the flu?

A. Drink more water.

B. Have a vaccine shot.

C. Drink healthy fluids.

(　　) 4. Who can easily have flu?

A. Children and the elderly.

B. People with any other illness.

C. Both A and B.

(　　) 5. What should we do if we get the flu or a cold?

A. Drink plenty of water.

B. Get plenty of rest.

C. Both A and B.

Writing （Task 12，共10分）

Task 12

Serving others can bring us happiness. The summer holiday is coming, and you'll go to the community to do some volunteer work. Write your plan according to the information below. (10 points) 服务他人，快乐自己。暑假即将来临，你计划去社区做一些志愿服务工作。请根据以下信息，写出你的计划。

Place	Activities
community centre	help the elderly, sing songs, tell stories...
community hospital	hand out the leaflets (宣传册) on how to keep healthy...
community park	pick up rubbish, water flowers...
...	...

As we all know, "Serving others can bring us happiness." The summer holiday is coming. I'll ______________________________

____

____

____

____

I'm sure I'll have a meaningful holiday this summer.

（二）

Speaking （Task 1–Task 3，共20分）

Task 1

You are a doctor. Now you are giving some advice on how to prevent colds. Read the following advice loudly. (0.5×10=5 points) 你是一名医生，正在告诉大家一些预防感冒的建议。请将以下建议大声读出来。

1. drink more water
2. wash hands
3. do sport
4. open the window
5. eat more vegetables
6. eat more fruit
7. wear a mask
8. keep the room clean
9. get enough sleep
10. keep a safe distance from the sick

Task 2

You are Li Hua, working in ABC Company. Now you are talking with your colleague Penny about shopping. Read the conversation loudly and tell others your opinion. (5 points) 你叫李华，在ABC公司工作。你正和同事彭妮谈论购物的话题。请大声读出对话，告诉大家你的想法。

Penny: Excuse me, Li Hua. Could you please give me a hand?

Li Hua: OK. Are these packages all yours? You have bought a lot of things.

Penny: Yes, they are all mine. I bought them online during the Double Eleven shopping festival. They are cheaper than usual.

Li Hua: Yeah, they're cheaper. But are they necessary for you? You can just buy the things that you really need.

Penny: You are right. Next time I'll make a shopping list. Thanks for your advice.

Li Hua: You're welcome.

Task 3

You are a teacher in a primary school. Now you are sharing your ideas about smartphones with your students. Read your opinion loudly. (10 points) 你是一位小学老师，正在与学生分享你对智能手机的看法。请大声读出你的观点。

> What's the greatest invention for you? Someone may say "smartphones". In my opinion, I also think the smartphone is one of the greatest inventions. A smartphone can be used as a wallet, a camera, a TV set, a computer, even the key to a car. It makes life really convenient. You can keep in touch with others by using smartphones. If you want to get some information from the Internet, just take out your smartphone. But please remember one thing: Do not use smartphones for too long.

Listening （Task 4–Task 6，共20分）

Task 4

You are Joe, and you are calling Wu Lin on the phone to talk about the weekend plan. You are going to hear five questions from Wu Lin. Listen carefully and respond. Each question will be read twice. (1×5=5 points) 你是乔，正在给吴琳打电话，想讨论周末的计划。你会听到吴琳的5个问题。请听提问并做出回应。每个问题读两遍。

(　　) 1. A. Hi, this is Joe.
B. Hi, I am Joe.
C. Hi, it's Joe.

(　　) 2. A. Do you want to play basketball with me tomorrow?
B. It's a basketball.
C. Hi, Jerry.

(　　) 3. A. How about 9:00 am?
B. How about at the playground?
C. How about you?

(　　) 4. A. Shall we meet at the gym?
B. Shall we meet at 3:00 pm?
C. Shall we meet tomorrow?

(　　) 5. A. Sure.
B. See you then.
C. Let's go.

Task 5

Jane and Mike are desk-mates. In class, Ms Zhang asks students to express their opinions about their favourite invention. Now, they are talking about it with each other. Choose the right information according to the conversation. The conversation will be read twice. (1×5=5 points) 简和迈克是同桌。上课时，张老师让大家讨论对最爱的发明的看法。现在，他们俩正在谈论各自喜爱的发明。请根据对话内容选择正确信息。对话读两遍。

(　　) 1. What's Jane's favourite invention?
A. Something useful.　B. The e-book reader.　C. The smartphone.

(　　) 2. Why does Jane like it?
A. Because she can do a lot of things with it.
B. Because Mike likes it.
C. Because it has changed her reading habit so much.

(　　) 3. What's Mike's favourite invention?
A. The smartphone.　B. The e-book reader.　C. Something useful.

(　　) 4. Why does Mike like it?
A. Because there are so many inventions.
B. Because he can read with it wherever he is.
C. Because it is cheap.

(　　) 5. Who wants to invent something useful someday?
A. Jane.　B. Mike.　C. Not sure.

Task 6

Wu Lin has bought some snacks. Now he is paying his bill. Listen to the conversation between Wu Lin and the cashier, and fill in the information. The conversation will be read twice. (2×5=10 points) 吴林购买了零食，现在他正在付账。请听他和收银员的对话，并填写信息。对话读两遍。

Item	Quantity	Unit price
Bread	5	3. ________ *yuan*
French fries	10	4. ________ *yuan*
Chocolate	1. ________	28 *yuan*
Juice	2. ________	7 *yuan*
Total		5. ________ *yuan*

Reading（Task 7–Task 11，共50分）

Task 7

You are talking about your family activities with your friends. Match the activities to the pictures. (2×5=10 points) 你正在和朋友谈论家庭活动。请将下列活动与对应的图片配对。

A. take pictures　　B. go travelling　　C. climb a mountain

D. do sport　　E. go camping

1. ________

2. ________

3. ________

4. ______________

5. ______________

1. ______________ 2. ______________ 3. ______________
4. ______________ 5. ______________

Task 8

You are talking about your schedule of next Saturday with your friends. Complete the schedule according to your plan. (2×5=10 points) 你正和朋友谈论自己下周六的安排。请根据以下安排，填写日程表。

Next Saturday is my mother's birthday. I will have a lot of things to do that day. I will get up at 6:30 am and spend one hour doing sport, and having breakfast. I think it is good to get up early. Because I can have enough time to do sport and have breakfast. Then I will go out to meet my friends at the Zoo Café at 9:00 am. We will go to the shopping centre and have lunch there. I'd like to buy a birthday cake and a scarf for my mum. In the afternoon, I will take my mum out to see a film. I have bought the tickets. The film will be on at 2:45 pm. It's a moving film. I think my mum will like it. After that, we will have dinner in a restaurant. I will give her the scarf and the birthday cake.

Schedule

Time	Activities
6:30 am	get up
6:30 am to 1. ______	do sport and 2. ______ breakfast

9:00 am	3. _______ at a café, go to the shopping centre and buy 4. _______ and a scarf
2:45 pm	see a film with 5. _______

Task 9

You are Wang Gang, and you are travelling in Chongqing. You'd like to write a postcard to your friend Mike. Finish the postcard according to the travel plan. (1×10=10 points) 你是王刚，正在重庆旅游。你想给好朋友迈克写一张明信片。请根据下列旅行计划，完成明信片。

Travel plan	
Destination: Chongqing	Weather: hot and wet
Where to visit: Hongya Cave; Gele Mountain	What to eat: hot pot; noodles

Postcard

Dear Mike,

Greetings from Chongqing!

Chongqing is 1. _______ amazing city. It's hot and wet these days. I dislike the weather here. 2. _______ I love the food and scenery. This morning, I didn't go out and 3. _______ (stay) at the hotel because 4. _______ the rain. I felt really 5. _______ (bore) because I had nothing to do but sleep and watch TV. Luckily, it stopped 6. _______ (rain) at noon. So I went out to eat something special for lunch—hot pot. There is a big 7. _______ (different) between Beijing hot pot and Chongqing hot pot. The food here is really hot and spicy. Chongqing is famous 8. _______ hot pot. After lunch, I enjoyed 9. _______ (walk) around the city. I will visit Gele Mountain and Hongya Cave tomorrow. I will have noodles tomorrow morning and then go to Gele Mountain. Many people say Hongya Cave looks beautiful in the evening. So I will go to visit it in the evening. I'm sure I will enjoy myself and you will like it, 10. _______.

Yours,

Wang Gang

Task 10

You are the chairman of the student union in Sunshine School. You are talking about the volunteer work and answering the questions. (2×5=10 points) 你是阳光学校的学生会主席，正在介绍即将举行的志愿活动并回答同学提问。

> Attention, please! Some volunteers are wanted for the International Volunteer Day which is on 5 December. We plan to do volunteer work at a children's home this Saturday. We are going to organise different activities. We will teach children how to draw, play games with them, and hold a puppet show this Saturday. If you are ready to help and have free time this Saturday, welcome to join us. We are going to meet at the school gate at 8:00 am and come back to school before 5:00 pm. Thanks for your listening!

( ) 1. When is the International Volunteer Day?

A. 5 December. B. 15 December. C. 25 December.

( ) 2. Where are the volunteer activities going to be held this Saturday?

A. At a nursing home. B. At a children's home. C. At a hospital.

( ) 3.What activities are going to be held?

A. Teach children how to draw.

B. Hold a puppet show.

C. Both A and B.

( ) 4. Who are welcome to join the volunteer work?

A. People who are ready to help and have free time this Saturday.

B. People who are busy with study and ready to help.

C. People who are interested in volunteer work.

( ) 5. Where are the volunteers going to meet this Saturday?

A. At the children's home.

B. At the school gate.

C. At the park gate.

Task 11

You are a tour guide. You are helping visitors make their travel plan. Complete the travel plan according to the following information. (2×5=10 points) 你是一名导游，正在给游客做旅游计划。请根据以下景点介绍，完成旅游计划。

Here are some great ideas for your travel plans.

Beijing, the capital city of China, has a very rich history. You can visit many places of interest, such as the Great Wall and the Summer Palace. There are many museums and theatres. You can taste the delicious Beijing Roast Duck.

Guilin is a city where you can get close to nature. There you can forget your worries beside the beautiful mountains and rivers. You will fall in love with Guilin Rice Noodles and Snail Rice Noodles.

Shanghai is a modern city. The streets are lined with cafés and shops. The Oriental Pearl Tower is one of the highest buildings in Asia, which is a symbol of Shanghai. *Xiaolongbao* is a typical traditional Shanghai-style food.

Chengdu is a relaxing city. You can drink tea and watch Sichuan Opera in a teahouse. Dujiangyan and Wuhou Shrine are famous scenic spots. Sichuan is full of delicacies, such as hot pot and noodles.

Travel plan		
Place	**Famous scenic spots**	**Special food**
Beijing	the Great Wall and the Summer Palace	1. _______
Guilin	beautiful mountains and rivers	Guilin Rice Noodles and 2. _______
3. _______	the Oriental Pearl Tower	*xiaolongbao*
Chengdu	Wuhou Shrine and 4. _______	5. _______ and noodles

Writing （Task 12，共10分）

Task 12

You are Wang Li, a tour guide of Good Times Travel Agency. Your friend Sarah wants to visit Sichuan. Write a brief introduction about Sichuan to her according to the following information. (10 points) 你是美好时光旅行社导游王莉。你的朋友萨拉想来四川游玩。请根据以下信息，给她写一封推介信。

An introduction about Sichuan	
Location (位置)	southwest of China
Places to visit	◆ Dujiangyan Irrigation System ◆ Jiuzhaigou ◆ Wolong National Nature Reserve
Famous products (特产)	◆ bamboo products ◆ Zhuyeqing tea
Delicacies (美食)	◆ hot pot ◆ noodles

Dear Sarah,

I'm really glad to tell you something about Sichuan. ____________________

____

____

____

____

____

I'm looking forward to your coming.

Yours sincerely,

Wang Li

（三）

Speaking（Task 1–Task 3，共20分）

Task 1

You are a volunteer in the community. You are showing some great inventions in recent years. Read the following inventions loudly. (0.5×10=5 points) 你是社区的一名志愿者，正在为大家介绍近年的一些伟大发明。请将以下发明大声读出来。

1. high-speed railway
2. e-payment
3. Internet
4. smartphone
5. colour TV
6. e-book
7. online shopping
8. touch screen
9. hybrid rice
10. solar lamp

Task 2

You are Li Qiang. You are having an interview at a company. Read the conversation and tell others about your interview. (5 points) 你叫李强，正在一家公司参加面试。请大声读出对话，分享你的面试。

HR: Good morning, Mr Li. Can you tell us something about yourself first?

Li Qiang: Yes. I'm a hard-working and patient man. And I'm ready to help others.

HR: Do you like to do a task by yourself or in a group?

Li Qiang: I'd rather cooperate with others, and get the job done by working together.

HR: What about your weakness?

Li Qiang: I'm a little shy.

HR: Thank you for being interested in our company. We'll contact you as soon as possible.

Task 3

You are Zhang Ting, a salesman in a car company. One month ago, your boss asked you to prepare for an important meeting. Read what you did loudly and find the problems. (10 points) 你是张挺，一家汽车公司的销售人员。一个月以前，你的老板让你准备一场重要的会议。请大声读出你的做法，找出问题。

> There is one month left. It's enough to prepare for the meeting. I have plenty of time to finish the task. Don't be nervous. Just play computer games. Two weeks later, I still have two weeks. Easy, easy, just take a break. Then there is one week left. But I think one week is enough, so let me have some fun first. Finally, there is just one day left. What should I do? I can't finish it!

Listening （Task 4–Task 6，共20分）

Task 4

You are seeing a doctor now. You are going to hear five questions from the doctor. Listen carefully and respond. Each question will be read twice. (1×5=5 points) 你正在看医生。你将听到医生的5个问题。请听提问并做出回应。每个问题读两遍。

( ) 1. A. Let me take a look.
B. I have a bad cough and a sore throat.
C. I have a problem.

( ) 2. A. In two days.
B. Last week.
C. For two days.

( ) 3. A. Yes, I also have a poor appetite.
B. Yes, I also have a cough.
C. Yes, I also have a sore throat.

( ) 4. A. Yes, I usually stay up late.
B. Yes, I usually feel tired.
C. Yes, I get lots of rest.

(　　) 5. A. Yes, you're welcome.

B. No, thanks a lot.

C. Yes, that's all right.

Task 5

You are a train conductor in Chongqing Railway Station. Now, Zhou Bo, a passenger, is buying train tickets. Choose the right information according to the conversation. The conversation will be read twice. (1×5=5 points) 你是重庆火车站的一名售票员。现在，旅客周波正在购买车票。请根据对话内容选择正确信息。对话读两遍。

(　　) 1. Which city will Zhou Bo go to?

A. Beijing.　　B. Shanghai.　　C. Chongqing.

(　　) 2. Which train will Zhou Bo take?

A. The train this morning.

B. The first train tomorrow morning.

C. The train at 10:45 am.

(　　) 3. When is the leaving time of the first train tomorrow morning?

A. 10:45 am.　　B. 11:45 am.　　C. 8:15 am.

(　　) 4. How much does a ticket cost?

A. 150 *yuan*.　　B. 250 *yuan*.　　C. 300 *yuan*.

(　　) 5. How many tickets does Zhou Bo buy?

A. Two.　　B. Three.　　C. One.

Task 6

You work in the Lost and Found Department in Chongqing Railway Station. A passenger is asking you to help find his missing item. Listen to the conversation and fill in the information. The conversation will be read twice. (2×5=10 points) 你在重庆火车站的失物招领处工作。一位旅客正在请你帮助他找回遗失的物品。请听对话并填写信息。对话读两遍。

Lost and found information

Name	1. ______
Date	6 May
Time	10:30 am
Place	waiting room
Item lost	a middle-size leather 2. ______
Colour	3. ______
Things in it	A wallet, some name cards and a 4. ______
Phone number	5. ______

Reading (Task 7–Task 11，共50分)

Task 7

You are a nurse in Children's Hospital. Now you are writing down the symptoms of the patients. Match the symptoms to the pictures. (2×5=10 points) 你是儿童医院的一名护士。现在你正在记录病人的症状。请将下列表示症状的词汇与对应图片配对。

A. have a toothache	B. have a fever	C. have a headache
D. have a cough	E. have a running nose	

1. ______________

2. ______________

3. ______________

4. ______________

5. ______________

1. ____________ 2. ____________ 3. ____________
4. ____________ 5. ____________

Task 8

You are a doctor and you are introducing how to take the medicine for the bad cold. Read the introduction and complete the form. (2×5=10 points) 你是一名医生，正在给病人介绍治疗重感冒的药品的用法。请阅读以下介绍并填写说明卡。

Here is the medicine for the bad cold. It should be taken three times a day after meals. According to the instructions, grown-ups should take two pills each time; children aged eight to fifteen take one pill each time, and children from the age of four to seven take half a pill each time. But it is not fit for children below the age of four. What's more, it must be stored in a cool place and used before 10 May 2024.

Instructions

Take the pills 1. __________ times a day after meals.
Grown-ups: two pills each time
Children (8-15 years old): one pill each time
Children (4-7 years old): 2. __________ a pill each time
NOT fit for children below the age of 3. __________
Notes: put them in a 4. __________
can't be used 5. __________ 10 May 2024

Task 9

You are Lily, a student majoring in Pre-school Education in a vocational school. You' d like to work as a kindergarten teacher. Write an application letter according to the ad. (1×10=10 points) 你是莉莉，一名职业学校学前教育专业的学生，想要应聘幼儿园老师岗位。请根据下列招聘广告，写一封求职信。

Kindergarten teachers wanted

Requirements:

1. Be good at singing, dancing, drawing, and so on
2. Be good at English
3. Have a strong sense of responsibility
4. Have good communication skills

All must possess valid teaching certificates.

Contact Mr Black at 13425643278.

Dear Sir/Madam,

I'm writing to apply 1. _________ the job as a teacher in your kindergarten. My name is Lily, eighteen years old. I will graduate 2. _________ a vocational school in July. My major is Pre-school Education.

During the past three years, I 3. _________ (study) many subjects, such 4. _________ English, Chinese, maths, and computer science. But my favourite subject is English. My English is much 5. _________ (good) than any other subject. I am also good at 6. _________ the piano. What's more, I have got the teaching certificate.

I am 7. _________ outgoing, lovely and patient person. I can communicate 8. _________ others well and do everything 9. _________ (careful). People say I am a responsible person, too.

Hope you can give me a chance. Please contact me 10. _________ 123@qq.com. Looking forward to your reply.

Yours sincerely,

Lily

Task 10

You are live streaming to sell goods in the online shop. Answer the following questions according to the information. (2×5=10 points) 你正在网上直播卖货。请根据货品信息，回答顾客的提问。

> Hello, everyone! Welcome to Happy Shop. Today I will introduce a dress to you. It is the best seller this month. It is the latest style. It is made of silk. When you wear the soft dress, you will feel comfortable. There are four colours for you to choose from: red, yellow, white and pink. Whether you are in the twenties or in the sixties, you can find the colour that suits you. We have different sizes, such as size S, size M and size L. The most important thing is its price. Though it is very popular, it is good value for money. Today there's a special 10% discount, so you only spend 180 *yuan* to take it. If you take two, I will give you a sun hat as a gift. Attractive, isn't it? Come on! Have a look and choose your favourite one.

(　　) 1. What is the dress made of?

A. Silk.　　B. Cotton.　　C. Cloth.

(　　) 2. How many colours are there to choose from?

A. Two.　　B. Three.　　C. Four.

(　　) 3. What are the sizes for this dress?

A. Size S and size M.

B. Size M and size L.

C. Size S, size M and size L.

(　　) 4. If I take one dress today, how much should I pay?

A. 200 *yuan*.　　B. 180 *yuan*.　　C. 160 *yuan*.

(　　) 5. What gift can I get if I take two dresses today?

A. A sun hat.　　B. A larger discount.　　C. A best seller.

Task 11

You are a technician in Hongxing Factory. Besides technology, you think having the spirit of craftsmanship is necessary. So you call on everyone to learn from others. Read the passage about the spirit of craftsmanship and complete the information card. (2×5=10 points) 你是红星工厂的一名技师。除技术外，你认为具有工匠精神也是必要的。所以你号召大家向其他优秀的人学习。请阅读以下有关工匠精神的文章并填写信息卡。

People are talking about the spirit of craftsmanship (工匠精神) nowadays. What does it exactly mean? Let's learn about craftsmen from the documentary (纪录片) *Master In Forbidden City* (《我在故宫修文物》).

Look at these antique clocks. How delicate they are! They're beautiful, aren't they? You know, thanks to antique restorers, we can appreciate these priceless treasures. Antique restorers are a group of craftsmen who work in the Palace Museum. Their job is to restore ancient cultural relics. Their job requires real attention to detail. These antique restorers are extremely skilled. They devote themselves entirely to their work and never show off. It is amazing to combine the ancient skills and modern technologies. In my opinion, innovation is the spirit of craftsmanship.

Antique restorers	
Who they are	a group of 1. __________ who work in the Palace Museum
What qualities they have	real 2. __________ to 3. __________ devote themselves 4. __________ to their work never 5. __________ off

Writing （Task 12，共10分）

Task 12

You are studying at Xinhua Vocational School. Next week, you'll take part in an English speech contest. You want to give a presentation on a great scientist. Complete your writing based on the following information. (10 points) 你是新

华职业学校的一名学生。下周，你将要参加一场英语演讲比赛，你想向大家介绍一位伟大的科学家。请根据以下信息完成有关这位科学家的介绍。

Tu Youyou	
Birth	born in Ningbo, Zhejiang province in 1930
Achievements	◆ found a cure for malaria, which has saved millions of lives globally ◆ was awarded the Nobel Prize and won the respect of the world
Efforts	◆ read hundreds of ancient medical texts in search of clues ◆ carried out thousands of experiments and even tested new drugs on herself
Qualities	◆ strong-willed and self-motivated

Hello, everyone. It's an honour for me to introduce a great scientist to you.

____

____

____

____

____

____

____

____

附　听力原文及答案

听力原文

高一篇

新课标理念下的听力专项检测范例

（一）

Task 1

Question 1: Hello, Wu Lin. Are you happy at your new school?

Question 2: Really? In what way is it different?

Question 3: What do you usually do in the workshops?

Question 4: Which class do you like best?

Question 5: Why is it your favourite class?

Task 2

1 **Woman:** *Excuse me. Could you tell me how to get to the nearest subway station?*

Man: *Sure. It's not far from here. Go straight ahead and you will see a café. Keep walking for two or three minutes, and then you will see the subway station.*

Q: *How will the woman most probably go to the nearest subway station?*

2 **Man:** *I heard that you know Lynn well. How did you become friends?*

Woman: *We met at the photography club. We often take photos outdoors together.*

Q: *How did the woman and Lynn become friends?*

3 **Man:** *The weather report said there would be lots of snow in the afternoon.*

Woman: *Well, I hope so. Otherwise, it would be impossible for us to ski.*

Q: *What season is it?*

4 ***Woman:*** *How do you celebrate the Spring Festival?*

Man: *We have a family reunion dinner, give lucky money, set off firecrackers and so on.*

Q: *Which festival are they talking about?*

5 ***Woman:*** *I heard Tim likes eating takeaways. Is it true?*

Man: *He used to eat takeaways for meals, but he has got rid of this habit.*

Q: *Does Tim eat takeaways now?*

Task 3

Waiter: *May I take your order, sir?*

Joe: *Well, I can't decide. Everything looks so yummy. Are there any specialties?*

Waiter: *How about the dish "Yu Xiang Rou Si"?*

Joe: *Could you tell me something about "Yu Xiang Rou Si"?*

Waiter: *Certainly. It is actually fish-flavoured pork slices.*

Joe: *That sounds nice. What would you recommend to go with it?*

Waiter: *I'd like to recommend the stir-fried green beans.*

Joe: *All right, I will take them both.*

Waiter: *OK, what would you like to drink?*

Joe: *Just a glass of orange juice.*

Waiter: *Please wait a minute. I'll be back with your order soon.*

（二）

Task 1

Question 1: When is the Mid-Autumn Festival?

Question 2: How do you usually celebrate the Mid-Autumn Festival?

Question 3: Cool! What does the mooncake symbolise?

Question 4: Is there anything else special about this festival?

Question 5: Could you tell me your plan for the upcoming Mid-Autumn Festival?

Task 2

1 ***Woman:*** *Dad, there's a typhoon forecast for the coming weekend. We should make preparations.*

Man: *That's right. I'll buy plenty of food and water—enough to last for a few days.*

Q: *What preparations will the man make?*

2 ***Man:*** *Hello, I'm Mike's father. I want to know if Mike is getting along with his new classmates.*

Woman: *Very well. Mike is a friendly and helpful boy. Everyone likes him.*

Q: *What might be the relationship between the speakers?*

3 ***Man:*** *Do you take a bus to work every day?*

Woman: *No. My office is too far away from my home, so I drive to work.*

Q: *How does the woman go to work?*

4 ***Woman:*** *What does your father do?*

Man: *He used to be a worker, but now he is a technician.*

Q: *What does the man's father do now?*

5 ***Woman:*** *What should we do to save the earth?*

Man: *We should use public transport instead of travelling by car, and always try to recycle waste. What's more, we should plant more trees.*

Q: *How many solutions are mentioned in the conversation?*

Task 3

Lily: *Hi, Li Wei. Long time no see. You look so refreshed.*

Li Wei: *Thanks. I quit playing video games recently and now do sport regularly.*

Lily: *Good for you! What sport do you do?*

Li Wei: *I'm a big fan of soccer. It's such a fun game to play and watch. I play soccer two or three times a week.*

Lily: *Your active life sounds cool!*

Li Wei: *I enjoy it. Have you taken part in any sport?*

Lily: *No, I'm too busy with my study.*

Li Wei: *Come on. Getting regular exercise can help you stay focused when studying.*

基于学科核心素养的综合检测任务

（一）

Task 4

Question 1: How did you become friends?

Question 2: How do you get along with Grace?

Question 3: What are the friendship rules between you and Grace?

Question 4: What is Grace like?

Question 5: What are friends for?

Task 5

1 **Woman:** *Do you want to go shopping with me this weekend?*
Man: *I'm afraid I can't. I am going to visit some old friends.*
Q: *What is the man's plan for this weekend?*

2 **Woman:** *How do people in Thailand celebrate the New Year?*
Man: *They splash water on each other.*
Q: *What activity do people in Thailand have in the New Year?*

3 **Woman:** *Could you tell me where I can try the hot pot?*
Man: *Chongqing! It's very famous for its hot pot.*
Q: *What are they talking about?*

4 **Woman:** *Hi, Mike. Have you heard the news about the typhoon?*
Man: *Yes. Lots of people are homeless.*
Q: *What natural disaster do we know from the conversation?*

5 **Woman:** *I see some new boxes in our school. Are they used for refuse-sorting?*
Man: *Yes. In this way, we can help reduce waste and protect the environment.*
Q: *What are they talking about?*

Task 6

Li Mei: *Excuse me. I am lost here. Could you tell me the way to the dining hall?*
Lin Tao: *Sure. It's not far from here. Go straight ahead, then turn left. Oh, it's just opposite the library.*

Li Mei: *You mean the building with the red roof?*

Lin Tao: *Yeah, that's it. The library is the most beautiful building in our school.*

Li Mei: *How long will it take to get to the dining hall?*

Lin Tao: *It's about three minutes.*

Li Mei: *Oh, I see. By the way, is there a supermarket in the school?*

Lin Tao: *Yes, there is one. You can find it on the first floor of the dining hall.*

Li Mei: *Oh, that's helpful. Thank you very much.*

Lin Tao: *You are welcome.*

（二）

Task 4

Question 1: Excuse me. Can I take your order now?

Question 2: What would you like to start with?

Question 3: What would you like as the main course?

Question 4: How would you like your steak cooked?

Question 5: Anything to drink?

Task 5

1 **Woman:** *Where are you from?*

Man: *I am from Paris, the capital of France.*

Q: *Which city is the man from?*

2 **Man:** *How long will it take by subway?*

Woman: *It'll only take about half an hour. It's much faster than taking a bus.*

Q: *How long will it take by bus?*

3 **Man:** *Mum, there's a typhoon forecast for Sunday. We should make some preparations.*

Woman: *Buy some food and water, and I'll also check our basic medical supplies.*

Q: *Which is not mentioned in the conversation?*

4 **Woman:** *How do you celebrate the Mid-Autumn Festival?*

Man: *We eat mooncakes and enjoy the moon.*

Q: *Which festival are they talking about?*

5 ***Woman:*** *In what way is your school different?*

Man: *We have skill-training workshops.*

Q: *What kind of school is the man probably in?*

Task 6

Joe: *Excuse me. Can you tell me where Hongya Cave is?*

Wu Lin: *Sure. Go straight ahead. Turn right at the next street. You'll see a special building on the hillside and riverside. That's Hongya Cave and the entrance is on your right.*

Joe: *Do you mean that I go that way for one block, and then turn right?*

Wu Lin: *Yes, you are right.*

Joe: *Is it far?*

Wu Lin: *No. It's only about ten minutes' walk.*

Joe: *Thank you very much. By the way, could you also tell me if there are any interesting sights to see inside?*

Wu Lin: *Sure. There are many interesting places and you can enjoy the Chongqing-style life here.*

Joe: *That sounds great. Thank you for your help.*

Wu Lin: *You're welcome. Have a great day!*

（三）

Task 4

Question 1: Hi, Zhou Bo. How do you like your new school?

Question 2: In what way is your school different from a general school?

Question 3: What do you usually do in skill-training workshops?

Question 4: What's your favourite subject?

Question 5: Why do you like your favourite subject?

Task 5

1 ***Woman:*** *Excuse me. Can you tell me how much the T-shirt is?*

Man: *It's 9.15 dollars.*

Q: *How much is the T-shirt?*

2 ***Man:*** *Jane, are you going camping this weekend?*

Woman: *It depends on the weather. If it is sunny, we will go.*
Q: *Will Jane go camping this weekend?*

3 **Man:** *What's wrong with you?*
Woman: *I coughed for three days and have a fever now.*
Q: *Where does the conversation probably take place?*

4 **Woman:** *I love the weather. Neither too hot nor too cold.*
Man: *Yes, warm and clear.*
Q: *What is the weather like now?*

5 **Woman:** *I saw Lynn today. Guess what he does now?*
Man: *I know. He is doing business online.*
Q: *What does Lynn do now?*

Task 6

Joe: *Hi, Jane, this is Joe.*
Jane: *Hi, Joe. What's up?*
Joe: *I am sorry I will be a little bit late tonight. Remember I said earlier I would pick you up at 6:00? But I will meet you at 6:45 because I have to finish a report first.*
Jane: *OK. Don't worry. The film begins late. I'll wait.*
Joe: *Good. Get something to eat before I arrive.*
Jane: *I will.*

高二篇

新课标理念下的听力专项检测范例

（一）

Task 1

Question 1: Where is Chongqing located?
Question 2: What are people like in Chongqing?
Question 3: What is the most famous scenic spot in Chongqing?

Question 4: What about the weather in Chongqing?

Question 5: Could you tell us more about Chongqing?

Task 2

Jerry: *Hello, sir. Here is my appointment number.*

Doctor: *Hello, I'm Dr. Smith. Please take a seat.*

Jerry: *Thank you.*

Doctor: *What's the problem?*

Jerry: *I've got a terrible headache. I feel weak.*

Doctor: *How long have you been like this?*

Jerry: *For about two days.*

Doctor: *Let me have a check... Hmmm, I'm afraid you've got a cold.*

Jerry: *Is it serious?*

Doctor: *No, nothing serious. Take these medicines three times a day, drink more water, and rest at home. You'll feel better in a few days.*

Jerry: *I hope so. Thank you very much.*

Task 3

Wu Lin: *Hi, Han Yu! How's everything going? You seem pretty busy lately.*

Han Yu: *Hi, Wu Lin. Everything's pretty good. I am doing volunteer work at a children's home.*

Wu Lin: *That sounds interesting. What will the volunteers do?*

Han Yu: *There are different kinds of volunteer activities, such as playing games with children, chatting with the elderly and picking up rubbish.*

Wu Lin: *Are there any requirements for the volunteers?*

Han Yu: *Yes, the volunteers must be ready to help. They should also have good communication skills.*

Wu Lin: *OK, I'll apply too.*

（二）

Task 1

Question 1: What can I do for you?

Question 2: Which type of sports shoes do you prefer?

Question 3: What size do you wear?

Question 4: What colour do you like?
Question 5: What kind of payment do you use?

Task 2

Wang Lei: *Look! There are so many famous people in the pictures.*
Li Ying: *They are all respectable scientists and skilled craftsmen.*
Wang Lei: *Many of our classmates are fans of the scientists and craftsmen, like Yuan Longping, Tu Youyou and Gao Fenglin.*
Li Ying: *They are also the people I respect. They have contributed a lot to our country.*
Wang Lei: *I can't agree more. I will always be proud of Yuan Longping. He provided a solution to worldwide hunger.*
Li Ying: *Of course. He's my role model, too. I just want to be a professional person like him. He set a great example.*

Task 3

Lily: *Good morning, Professor Li's office. Can I help you?*
Visitor: *Good morning. I'd like to make an appointment with Professor Li.*
Lily: *OK. May I have your name and telephone number, please?*
Visitor: *Yes. This is Peter Brown. My number is 8053726. Would 9:00 tomorrow morning be all right?*
Lily: *I'm afraid not. He is going to give a speech in the morning.*
Visitor: *Oh, it is a pity! What's the earliest available time?*
Lily: *How about 7:00 pm tomorrow?*
Visitor: *That would be fine. Thank you very much.*
Lily: *It doesn't matter. Please come to the office 10 minutes early.*

基于学科核心素养的综合检测任务

（一）

Task 4

Question 1: Where are you from?
Question 2: How many people are there in Chongqing?
Question 3: What do you think of Chongqing people?

Question 4: Do you enjoy living in Chongqing?
Question 5: What is Chongqing famous for?

Task 5

Li Ying: *Hi, Jerry! How's everything going? You seem busy lately.*
Jerry: *Everything is good. I'm doing some volunteer work.*
Li Ying: *What volunteer work? What do you do there?*
Jerry: *I help out at a nursing home. We chat with the elderly and play games together.*
Li Ying: *How do the elderly feel?*
Jerry: *They are so happy to stay with us.*
Li Ying: *How do you feel at the nursing home?*
Jerry: *I'm happy, too. The elderly need to be taken good care of.*
Li Ying: *Wow, that's great. Can I join you? I want to help.*
Jerry: *You are welcome to join us!*

Task 6

Boss: *Mr Martin, a scientist from New York University, will arrive tomorrow. Please pick him up at the airport.*
Lily: *OK. When will Mr Martin arrive at the airport?*
Boss: *The plane will arrive at 5:30 pm tomorrow.*
Lily: *May I have his flight number?*
Boss: *The flight number is CA1409.*
Lily: *I see. Which hotel will he stay at?*
Boss: *Garden Hotel in the city centre.*
Lily: *OK. What should we do then?*
Boss: *We will hold a welcome party for him there tomorrow evening.*
Lily: *OK. I see.*

（二）

Task 4

Question 1: Hello? Who's that?
Question 2: Hi, Joe. What's up?
Question 3: When shall we meet?

Question 4: Where shall we meet?

Question 5: Can I invite my cousin to join us?

Task 5

Mike: *What's your favourite invention, Jane?*

Jane: *The smartphone, of course.*

Mike: *Why do you like it most?*

Jane: *I can do a lot of things with it, such as chatting with friends and taking photos. Is it also your favourite invention, Mike?*

Mike: *I'm afraid not. I like the e-book reader best.*

Jane: *Really? Why?*

Mike: *Well, I can read with it wherever I am. I can't live without it.*

Jane: *I see. There are so many inventions, and they have changed our lives so much.*

Mike: *That's true. I hope someday I can invent something useful.*

Jane: *Yeah. That would be cool.*

Task 6

Wu Lin: *So here are 5 loaves of bread, 10 bags of French fries, 4 boxes of chocolate and 5 bottles of juice.*

Cashier: *The bread is 10 yuan each loaf, the French fries 8 yuan each bag, the chocolate 28 yuan per box, and the juice 7 yuan each bottle. That adds up to 277 yuan.*

Wu Lin: *Can you deliver all these for me?*

Cashier: *Yes, we can deliver them for free.*

Wu Lin: *Thanks. Could I get the receipt now?*

Cashier: *Sure. Please wait a moment.*

（三）

Task 4

Question 1: Hello! What's wrong with you?

Question 2: When did your symptoms begin?

Question 3: Do you have any other symptoms?

Question 4: Do you usually stay up late?

Question 5: Take these tablets three times a day. And get lots of rest. You will feel better in a few days. Any questions?

Task 5

Conductor: *Can I help you?*

Zhou Bo: *Yes, please. I need to buy tickets. Could you tell me the time of the train to Shanghai this morning?*

Conductor: *I'm sorry that you have missed it. It left just ten minutes ago. You'll have to wait until tomorrow morning or go by bus.*

Zhou Bo: *I'll wait. When is the first train tomorrow morning?*

Conductor: *The first train leaves at 8:15 am and gets to Shanghai at 11:45 am. But it may be a little late because of the weather.*

Zhou Bo: *OK. How much does a ticket cost?*

Conductor: *250 yuan.*

Zhou Bo: *All right. I will take two tickets, please. Here's the money.*

Task 6

M: *Excuse me, Madam. Is this the Lost and Found Department?*

W: *Yes. Can I help you, sir?*

M: *I lost my bag at 10:30 am on 6 May in the waiting room. Could you help me find it?*

W: *Could you tell me what it looks like?*

M: *Let me see... It's a middle-size leather bag.*

W: *What colour is your bag?*

M: *Black.*

W: *OK. What's your name then?*

M: *Billy Newell. B-I-L-L-Y, Billy; N-E-W-E-L-L, Newell.*

W: *All right. B-I-L-L-Y, Billy; N-E-W-E-L-L, Newell. Is there anything important in it?*

M: *Oh, yes. A nice wallet and some name cards, and I put a new book in it. It's a present for my daughter's birthday.*

W: *I see, sir. We'll call you as soon as we find your missing bag.*

M: *Thank you, Madam. My phone number is 64892351.*

W: *All right, sir.*

答案

高一篇

新课标理念下的听力专项检测范例

（一）

Task 1

1. B　2. A　3. A　4. C　5. A

Task 2

1. B　2. B　3. C　4. A　5. B

Task 3

1. A　2. B　3. A　4. B　5. C

（二）

Task 1

1. A　2. C　3. C　4. A　5. B

Task 2

1. C　2. C　3. B　4. B　5. B

Task 3

1. B　2. C　3. A　4. C　5. A

新课标理念下的阅读专项检测范例

（一）

Task 1

1. C　2. A　3. E　4. B　5. D

Task 2

1. wealth　2. grapes　3. symbolises　4. success　5. better

Task 3

1. about　2. get up　3. have　4. bus　5. and

6. start/begin	7. in	8. workshop	9. sport	10. back

Task 4

1. A　2. A　3. C　4. C　5. B

Task 5

1. B　2. B　3. C　4. A　5. B

（二）

Task 1

1. C　2. E　3. D　4. B　5. A

Task 2

1. different	2. spicy	3. hot pot	4. Roast Goose	5. fresh

Task 3

1. from	2. if	3. with	4. about	5. interested
6. listener	7. an/your	8. friendly	9. bigger	10. making

Task 4

1. A　2. C　3. B　4. C　5. A

Task 5

1. A　2. B　3. C　4. B　5. A

新课标理念下的写作专项检测范例

略

基于学科核心素养的综合检测任务

（一）

Task 4

1. A　2. C　3. A　4. B　5. A

Task 5

1. B　2. C　3. A　4. A　5. B

Task 6

1. B　2. A　3. B　4. A　5. C

Task 7

1. D　2. E　3. B　4. A　5. C

Task 8

1. -5	2. Beijing	3. rainy	4. wear more clothes	5. sunny

Task 9

1. is	2. an	3. on	4. to invite	5. at
6. singing	7. be	8. happily	9. interested	10. seeing

Task 10

1. A　2. B　3. B　4. A　5. A

Task 11

1. fifth	2. Qu Yuan	3. *Zongzi*	4. popular	5. sport

Task 12

略

（二）

Task 4

1. A　2. A　3. B　4. A　5. C

Task 5

1. B　2. B　3. C　4. B　5. B

Task 6

1. B　2. A　3. A　4. A　5. B

Task 7

1. E　2. A　3. D　4. C　5. B

Task 8

1. vocational	2. workshops	3. kind	4. friendly	5. happy

Task 9

1. Which	2. in	3. play	4. If	5. choice
6. such as	7. well	8. writing	9. wait	10. make

Task 10

1. B　2. C　3. B　4. C　5. B

Task 11

1. C　2. B　3. B　4. C　5. C

Task 12

略

（三）

Task 4

1. A　2. A　3. C　4. B　5. B

Task 5

1. B 2. C 3. B 4. A 5. A

Task 6

1. A 2. B 3. B 4. C 5. A

Task 7

1. D 2. E 3. C 4. B 5. A

Task 8

1. green 2. changes 3. when 4. Second 5. more

Task 9

1. who 2. on 3. women's 4. making 5. medals
6. age 7. known 8. to 9. under 10. divers

Task 10

1. B 2. B 3. A 4. C 5. B

Task 11

1. C 2. B 3. C 4. C 5. C

Task 12

略

高二篇

新课标理念下的听力专项检测范例

（一）

Task 1

1. B 2. B 3. C 4. C 5. A

Task 2

1. A 2. B 3. C 4. A 5.C

Task 3

1. children's 2. playing games 3. picking 4. ready 5. communication

（二）

Task 1

1. B 2. C 3. B 4. A 5. A

Task 2

1. A 2. B 3 .C 4. A 5. C

Task 3

1. morning 2. Peter 3. 7:00 pm 4. speech 5. office

新课标理念下的阅读专项检测范例

（一）

Task 1

1. E 2. C 3. B 4. A 5. D

Task 2

1. speed 2. without 3. that 4. used 5. completely

Task 3

1. 20 2. in 3. when 4. with 5. keep
6. balanced 7. and 8. enough 9. getting 10. advised

Task 4

1. B 2. B 3. C 4. A 5. A

Task 5

1. A 2. B 3. C 4. A 5. C

（二）

Task 1

1. C 2. D 3. E 4. B 5. A

Task 2

1. April 2. wars 3. good luck 4. 1984 5. fireworks shows

Task 3

1. are 2. first 3. that/which 4. best 5. delicious
6. another 7. best 8. more 9. Although/Though 10. of

Task 4

1. A 2. C 3. B 4. A 5. C

Task 5

1. A 2. B 3. B 4. C 5. C

新课标理念下的写作专项检测范例

略

基于学科核心素养的综合检测任务

（一）

Task 4

1. B 2. B 3. C 4. A 5. A

Task 5

1. A 2. B 3. C 4. A 5. C

Task 6

1. scientist 2. 5:30 pm 3. CA1409 4. Garden 5. welcome

Task 7

1. E 2. D 3. B 4. C 5. A

Task 8

1. 1994 2. social services 3. 1904 4. peace 5. a better place

Task 9

1. and 2. coming 3. in 4. are invited 5. was
6. elderly 7. more 8. Another 9. that/which 10. useful

Task 10

1. C 2. B 3. A 4. A 5. C

Task 11

1. C 2. C 3. B 4. C 5. C

Task 12

略

（二）

Task 4

1. A 2. A 3. A 4. A 5. A

Task 5

1. C 2. A 3. B 4. B 5. B

Task 6

1. 4 2. 5 3. 10 4. 8 5. 277

Task 7

1. E 2. B 3. A 4 .C 5. D

Task 8

1. 7:30 am 2. have 3. meet friends 4. a birthday cake 5. my mum

Task 9

1. an	2. But	3. stayed	4. of	5. bored
6. raining	7. difference	8. for	9. walking	10. too

Task 10

1. A　2. B　3. C　4. A　5. B

Task 11

1. Beijing Roast Duck　2. Snail Rice Noodles　3. Shanghai
4. Dujiangyan　5. hot pot

Task 12

略

（三）

Task 4

1. B　2. B　3. A　4. A　5. B

Task 5

1. B　2. B　3. C　4. B　5. A

Task 6

1. Billy Newell	2. bag	3. black	4. new book	5. 64892351

Task 7

1. D　2. E　3. B　4. A　5. C

Task 8

1. three	2. half	3. four	4. cool place	5. after

Task 9

1. for	2. from	3. have studied	4. as	5. better
6. playing	7. an	8. with	9. carefully	10. at

Task 10

1. A　2. C　3. C　4. B　5. A

Task 11

1. craftsmen	2. attention	3. detail	4. entirely	5. show

Task 12

略